The Manager's Pocket Guide to

Leadership Skills

Peter B. Stark
and
Jane Flaherty

HRD Press
Amherst, Massachusetts

Published by:

HRD Press, Inc.
22 Amherst Road
Amherst, MA 01002
1-800-822-2801 (U.S. and Canada)
413-253-3488
413-253-3490 (FAX)
www.hrdpress.com

 PRINTED IN CANADA

ISBN 0-87425-472-8

Cover illustration by Meg McCarthy
Cover design by Eileen Klockars
Editorial services by Robie Grant
Production services by Clark Riley

TABLE OF CONTENTS

Dedication

We would like to acknowledge the many employees and members of management teams who have contributed to our knowledge and understanding of effective leadership in organizations. Your insights and candid feedback are the seeds of wisdom in formulating this book.

Specifically, our appreciation goes to the employees and managers we have worked with at the following organizations: Accredited Home Lenders, Action Instruments, American Residential Mortgage Corporation/Chase Manhattan, American Specialty Health Plans, Association of Legal Administrators, Campbell Sales Company, Carlson Companies, Chromalloy, Chula Vista Elementary School District, City of Oceanside, County of San Diego, Eagle Creek Travel Gear, Entergy Operations, Foodmaker Inc., Grossmont Bank, Hallmark Circuits, Hewlett Packard, Institute of Management Studies, La Jolla Beach and Tennis Club, Lightspan Partnership, Los Angeles Dodgers, MailBoxes Etc., Mission Federal Credit Union, Motorola, National Basketball Association, NCR, North Island Federal Credit Union, PETCO, Portland Trail Blazers, Princess Cruises, Quintiles, Ralston Purina, San Diego Convention Center, San Diego Padres, San Diego State University, Texas Utilities, Unisys, University of Phoenix, US Department of Defense, Wisconsin Electric, and Xerox.

Preface

No matter how you arrived at your supervisory position, you will need a specific set of skills to work successfully with your employees. Feeling positive about yourself, making effective decisions, and solving problems will still be a part of your daily life. Added to this will be the significant and challenging leadership skills of communicating, delegating, coaching, motivating, hiring, and leading.

Your achievement will now be measured by your staff's performance. Knowing how to work with your staff will increase your department's effectiveness. And, your employees can become your best support as you become one of today's successful leaders.

The Manager's Pocket Guide to Leadership Skills concisely describes the skills you will need to become a strong and competent supervisor and manager. This book contains information and illustrations, as well as "Tips for Success" and "Action Plans." It is written for those who want to not only survive, but thrive in their leadership role!

Introduction

Over the last 20 years, we have had the opportunity to read hundreds of books on leadership, supervision, and management. Each of the books we invested in seemed to have ideas we were able to use in our managerial careers, as well as share with our business clients. So, it would seem that the last thing we need is another book on supervising and managing employees!

However, there are three reasons we have taken the time to put our thoughts on paper. First, after having the opportunity to train thousands of new and experienced supervisors and managers, we feel we have a solid understanding of what skills it takes to be a successful leader in today's business environment.

Second, we wanted to concentrate on the personal and people skills required to be a great leader. We have found that most people in supervisory, managerial, or other positions of leadership have extremely strong technical skills. In fact, people are usually hired and promoted based on how well they do the "operational" functions of a position. Although strong in technical skills, our experience has found that most people in positions of authority are not equally strong in their people skills. To continue up the ladder of organizational success, we must be willing to "fine-tune" relationship-building skills. This book concentrates on these necessary skills.

Third, we wanted to write something on supervision that people would want to read. *The Manager's Pocket Guide to Leadership Skills* is a shortened, concise version of *The Competent Manager* (HRD Press, 1999). We hope this book will provide you with enough information to improve your skills in managing and leading people, as well as be easy to read. Although the reading is intended to be easy, building the skills and going through the associated growth process described in each chapter will be challenging. It will take hard work on your part.

We use the term supervisor and manager interchangeably. Our reasoning for doing so is twofold. First, we have found little consistency in how organizations decide whether someone is a manager or a supervisor. In one organization, a person with certain responsibilities may be called a supervisor, but in another organization, a person with the same responsibilities may be called a manager—or even a vice president. The second reason we overlap the terms is that we believe the people-related skills required by both supervisors and managers—and even vice presidents—are identical. The responsibilities may be significantly different, but the people-related skills are basically the same.

As we share our ideas, it is important to realize this book for what it is: insight from two consultants on the skills needed to be a great supervisor or manager. We are the first to agree that the information will not work in every situation. You will have to adapt the material to meet your unique needs and situations. At the same time, we are also convinced that if managers and supervisors would apply the skills we have described, they would eliminate about 90% of the consulting work we do today in most organizations!

The bottom line: The skills presented here will work, if you are willing to learn and then practice them. If you are willing to invest the reading time, as well as the skill-building practice on the job, we promise that you will be proud of the results. You and your employees will accomplish more...and everyone will gain more enjoyment from working together. We wish you success!

P.S. When you do a better job as a supervisor, you will also sleep better at night!

1

Understanding the Changing Role of Supervison

"Predicting the future is easy. It's trying to figure out what's going on now that's hard."
Fritz R. S. Dressler

A bewildered manager recently said in one of our seminars, "I just don't get it...what's going on with today's employees? What is it they want?" Seasoned managers, those with 20 to 30 years of experience, unanimously agree on one issue: the role of the 21st century manager and the skills required to get the job done today are significantly different from the role of the supervisor/manager of the 1940s and 1950s. This initial chapter briefly reviews some of the reasons that contribute to this changing role.

Environmental and Economic Changes

One of the best ways to determine how the role of the supervisor has changed is to study how organizations are being impacted by changes in the environment and the economy.

1. **The most notable shift in our environment has been from an industrial-based society to an information-based society.** In 1980, the amount of information entering our society was doubling every ten years. In 1990, the amount of information entering society was doubling every two and one-half years! As we near the year 2000, it is estimated that the amount of information will double every one and one-half years!

2. **The rapid increase in information flow is both creating new jobs and causing jobs to become obsolete.** It has been estimated that 50% of the jobs being performed in 1991 did not exist in 1971. That rate of change is not slowing down. We can expect that by the year 2013 essentially all work will be "new." If information is doubling every one and one-half years, 90 percent of the information available to workers in 2013 will have been created since 1993. Put another way, all of the knowledge utilized by workers in 1993 represents 10% of what will be available in 20 years.

3. **Our economy has shifted from a manufacturing base to a service base.** In 1955, according to an analysis done by Morgan Guaranty Trust Company, manufacturing produced some 30% of all U.S. goods. In 1985, this figure dropped to 21%. By the year 2000, it is expected to drop to 17%. As this happens, manufacturing will become less and less important to the economy as a mechanism for

creating wealth. Although there will be fewer manufacturing jobs in 2000, these losses will be more than offset by net new jobs in the service sector.

4. **Global competition is changing the way we do business.** In the 1940s and 1950s, American-made products were symbolic of high quality. Today, we are struggling to maintain our competitive edge. Presently, 80% of what any organization produces can be equaled by other organizations in the world. Businesses can now choose to compete because access to the information, knowledge, raw materials, and technologies needed to do the core, repetitive tasks is available to anyone who wants it, many times from the Internet.

5. **Environmental consciousness and practices are required.** It is virtually impossible to ignore the strong emphasis being placed on environmental consciousness. Corporations must comply with new environmental regulations every year.

6. **Technological advances are coming faster than ever before.** Technology is advancing so rapidly it is difficult for even the experts to keep up. A computer specialist was asked, "How can consumers be sure that they are getting a 'state-of-the-art' computer?" The computer technician's interesting reply was, "If a computer has progressed enough for us to sell it on the retail market, it's already obsolete!"

3

The computer has changed the way we do business. Access to the Internet has leveled the playing field by giving anyone with a computer and a modem a powerful tool to conduct research, advertise products, and stay current with the latest in just about anything!

7. **Laws, laws, and more legal stuff.** Legal issues are an ongoing and growing concern for organizations. From the employee lawsuits regarding workplace harassment and equal opportunity, to laws that dictate the particulars for how we do business, the legal process has affected almost everyone. As organizations struggle to interpret the intent and impact of laws governing the workplace, policies have changed considerably.

Workforce Composition Changes

In addition to environmental and economic changes, our workforce has also dramatically changed. Several major trends have contributed to this new workforce.

1. **In the last 50 years, the most significant change in our workforce has been the number of women on the job.** In the 1950s, less than 35% of American women worked outside the home. In 1960, less than 40% of them did. But, the social changes of the late 1960s and early 1970s, coupled with genuine financial necessity, allowed women to gain a foothold in the business world. By 1985, 61%

4

of all married women with children were part of the labor force—more than twice the 1960 rate of 28%. This trend is continuing. By the year 2000, it is estimated by the Department of Labor that about 48% of the workforce will be female.

2. **The average age of the workforce is increasing.** Between now and the year 2000, the number of workers between the ages of 35 and 54 will increase by more than 25 million, and the median age for employed Americans will rise to 45 years, up from 36 years in 1987. By the year 2005, more than 15% of the workforce will be over age 55. Never before has such a large segment of our workforce been so near to retirement age.

3. **The number of available workers is decreasing.** Today many employers are finding themselves in the unaccustomed position of scrambling for workers. Between now and the year 2000, the number of young workers aged 16 to 24 will drop by almost two million, or 8%. This decline is already affecting many businesses. Companies in the service industries, such as fast-food restaurants and hotels, are experiencing increasing difficulty in hiring and retaining employees.

4. **The number of minorities in the workplace will continue to increase.** By the year 2000, members of American minority groups— especially African-Americans and Hispanics—

will be less of a minority in the workforce than ever before. According to the U.S. Bureau of Labor Statistics in 1993, by the end of this century, African-Americans will make up over 12% of the total workforce; Hispanics will account for 10%, and Asians another 4%. Over the next several years, almost one-third of all new entrants into the labor force will be minorities—twice their current share.

5. **The education gap is widening.** The United States currently has the most highly educated workforce in its history. In 1964, 45.1% of workers had high school diplomas. As recently as the late 1980s, 86% of 25- to 29-year-olds had high school diplomas. Never before have more people in the workforce attended college. Estimates are that by the year 2000, at least half of our workforce will have some college education. On the other hand, the number of people who are considered functionally illiterate continues to increase. While it is difficult to accurately measure illiteracy, estimates claim approximately 20 million people are illiterate. Approximately 25% of those who graduate from high school cannot read past the eighth-grade level.

6. **Workers are packing up and going.** Fifty years ago, packing up your family and moving was a big deal. In the 1940s and 1950s, changing jobs was unusual. Statistics tell us our parents probably had only two or three distinct careers. We will probably have five to six. Our children

will probably have eight to ten different careers, six of which have not even been conceived yet!

These workforce trends make it even more difficult to be a successful supervisor. Aside from getting the job done, other issues arise: a worker who is older than the supervisor, a worker who does not understand English or does not read well, a worker who has more formal education than the manager, and co-workers who encounter cultural conflicts. Perhaps most significantly of all, there are many men still unsure how to relate to women in the workplace.

Changing Workforce Values

One of the most striking ways to study how the role of the supervisor has changed over the last 50 years is to look at the values of the workers they supervise. A list of typical work values in the 1940s and 1950s is illustrated below, as well as some of the critical values of today's workforce. What a contrast!

Looking at the two lists of values, it becomes clear that today's worker is no longer happy to just have a job. Today's workers not only want work to be meaningful and fun, they want to be recognized for their contributions. This need for job fulfillment is expressed not only by workers, but by supervisors and managers themselves.

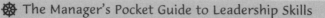

Values of the Workforce Past and Present

Values of the 1940s-1950s Workforce	Values of Today's Workforce
Family	Benefits
Good craftsmanship	Concern for health
Happy to have a job	Education
Job stability	Flexible schedule
Loyalty to boss	High concern for self
Loyalty to company	Input appreciated
Patriotism	Interesting work
Savings account	Need for time off
Technical ability	Open communication
	Opportunity to advance
	Personal growth
	Recognition

Occasionally, we hear disgruntled managers say, "Workers today have no values!" Typically, the manager, a Baby Boomer who worked long, hard hours to get where he or she is today, has difficulty understanding Generation X's priorities, which include the need to be recognized; workplace flexibility; equality among team members; and an employer who recognizes the employee's need to have a balanced life. Simply put, employees born between 1960 and 1980 who are now in, or just entering, the workforce have very different values than the previous generation.

While there may be a tendency on the part of the manager to discount these values as being "soft," self-serving, or not loyal to the employer, taking a quick look at the facts will help us understand why today's workers are bringing with them a very different set of values.

First, we jokingly say employees today listen to radio station "W.I.I.F.M." or, "What's in it for me?" Workers are keenly interested in how much you pay and what benefits you offer. They see themselves as providing you, the employer, with a needed commodity, and want to be fairly paid for what they offer. Some harsh economic facts are driving Generation X's financial concerns. According to Claire Raines in her 1997 book, *Beyond Generation X,* the following conditions are faced by young employees today:

> Poverty among "twenty-somethings" has increased by 50% since the mid-1970s.
>
> In the 1950s, young homeowners could make the monthly mortgage payment by using 14% of their income. Today it takes 40%.
>
> Americans work an average of one month per year more than they did ten years ago, yet real wages have steadily declined since 1973.
>
> Home ownership may be unrealistic for many members of Generation X. The median price of a home (adjusted for inflation) has increased 78% in the last 30 years.
>
> In the 1960s, one of ten college graduates took jobs that didn't require their degrees. Over the next 15 years, one in three graduates will have to settle for jobs that don't match their credentials.

Fortune 500 companies are laying off workers at an unprecedented pace. The trend is expected to worsen in the next century.

In addition to financial challenges, younger employees look to the future they will be inheriting and see pollution, crime, racial tension, and AIDS, leading to a sense of powerlessness. Experienced managers often see these skeptical employees as "jaded" and note they don't share the same sense of optimism that the manager did when he or she started working.

Perhaps one of the most difficult aspects for today's manager, though, is this generation's lack of respect for authority and limited interest in titles. This generation was the first to grow up, under the guidance of Dr. Spock, in an egalitarian home atmosphere. Both parent and child had rights and provided input into family affairs. Further, this was the first generation that spent long hours on their own, after school, waiting for parents to return home after work. The ability to "fend for themselves" has resulted in a more self-reliant, autonomous employee.

Based on these values, what skills did it take for a supervisor in the 1940s and 1950s to manage their workers effectively? If the worker was loyal to the boss, loyal to the company, and thankful to have a job, the skills needed to manage might look like those outlined below. Based on today's values, review the skills needed to be a successful manager in today's world.

Skills to Manage
Employees Past and Present

Skills Needed: 1940s-1950s Supervisor	Skills Needed: Today's Supervisor
Ability to control Delegation Directive Problem solving Strong authority figure Technical expertise	Clarifying expectations Coaching and counseling Communication Confidence Consulting Creativity Delegating Enabling Empowering Leadership Listening Mentoring Motivating Negotiation Organizing Problem solving Questioning Team building

How is that for a list of what is required for supervisors to do their jobs effectively? Ten years ago we could look at the list of what today's workers want and agree that it would be nice if we could provide a work environment like that. We might even agree that it would theoretically be the right thing to do. Today, however, we are faced with a new reality, and that is, if you are managing a business where the majority of your front-line employees are members of Generation X, your business will not be successful, and may not even survive, unless you manage them well.

Given the changing values employees bring with them to the workplace, coupled with the fact that it has become increasingly more difficult to hire qualified employees in the late 1990s (and incredibly expensive to replace them when they leave), it makes sense that effectively managing the workers of today is not optional, it is mandatory.

The challenge for all supervisors today is to gain the attention, trust, enthusiasm, and commitment of their employees. It is no longer adequate to assemble, organize, and manage capital, raw materials, and a workforce within a tightly defined system of production. What is required is the leadership skill to create work environments of creativity, innovation, and enthusiasm so that once hired, our employees are committed, loyal, and stay with us.

In Chapters Two and Three, we will discuss the skills that help build relationships, encourage motivated employees, and foster a creative environment. The remaining chapters are devoted to enhancing your skills to become a confident, successful leader in today's environment.

2

Building Your Confidence and Self-Esteem

"Our own attitudes have far more to do with how happy we are than do any external circumstances."
Dr. Nathaniel Branden

Being a great supervisor starts with you. The way you feel and see yourself affects every aspect of your role as a leader. William James, the great philosopher and psychologist, once observed that the greatest discovery of our age has been that we, by changing the inner aspects of our thinking, can change the outer aspects of our life. Or as another sage puts it, "We aren't what we think we are, but what we think, we are!" The higher your self-esteem, the better your chances are of being a great supervisor and a great leader. This chapter discusses the importance of self-esteem and what you can do to raise your self-esteem to an even higher level.

As a first step to enhancing self-esteem, we can begin with a self-assessment. This is an opportunity for you to take an honest look at yourself and assess how you feel about your abilities as a supervisor. In which aspects of supervision do you have a high degree of confidence? In which aspects are you unsure or feel a lack of confidence? The Self-Esteem Assessment below gives you a starting point to determine your strengths as a supervisor and leader, as well as providing a springboard for setting goals and improving skills.

Self-Esteem Assessment

On a scale of 1 to 10 (10 being the highest confidence score, 5 being an average confidence score, and 1 being the lowest or no confidence score), rate how you feel about yourself in each of the 16 areas. Use any number between 1 and 10 to accurately describe your feelings. For example, if you feel just slightly above average on your communication skills as a supervisor, you might rate them as a 6, but if you feel more confident, rate them as an 8.

As a supervisor, I feel the following levels of confidence in each category, ranging from 1 to 10, (10 being the highest level of confidence).

1. ____ My relationship with people who report to me.

2. ____ My relationship with my boss.

3. ____ My verbal communication skills.

4. ____ My written communication skills.

5. ____ My technical skills to get the job done.

6. ____ My ability to motivate others.

7. ___ My ability to solve problems in my department as they arise.

8. ___ My ability to coach and counsel people so they improve their performance.

9. ___ My relationships with co-workers.

10. ___ My ability to organize my tasks and my work area effectively.

11. ___ My ability to accomplish my organizational goals.

12. ___ My ability as a leader.

13. ___ Others' level of trust in me.

14. ___ My level of trust in my employees.

15. ___ My ability to interview and hire the right people.

16. ___ My ability to delegate tasks and responsibilities effectively.

Next, identify your top three areas of strength and your three areas for improvement.

Areas of Strength	Areas for Improvement
1.	1.
2.	2.
3.	3.

What Is Self-Esteem?

Self esteem is quite simply how you feel about yourself. How we feel about ourselves critically influences virtually every aspect of our lives. Our self-esteem influences everything from the way we function at work, to our personal relationships, to our role as parents, to what we accomplish in life. Every response we make in life and every goal we set, is shaped by whom and what we think we are. Thus, self-esteem is the major key to our success, our failure, and the level of our accomplishment as a supervisor or leader.

Self-esteem has two components: (1) a feeling of personal competence and (2) a feeling of personal worth. In other words, self-esteem is the sum of our self-confidence and self-respect. Self-esteem, on whatever level, is an intimate experience; it resides in the core of our being. It is what you think and feel about yourself, not how someone else thinks or judges you.

The tragedy related to self-esteem is that so many people look for self-confidence and self-respect everywhere except within themselves, and so they fail in their search. Unless you perceive your own true worth as a person or supervisor, you cannot come close to achieving high self-esteem. Only to the degree that you can truly acknowledge your own unique importance will you be able to free yourself from self-imposed limitations.

What Are the Benefits of High Self-Esteem?

With poor self-csteem, life can be difficult at its best. Fortunately, we can improve our self-esteem. If you are willing to take the time to work at developing your self-esteem, there are many benefits.

You will feel happier about life. When you feel more positive about yourself, it is only natural that you will be able to cope with life and its interesting twists and turns better. When you have high self-esteem, you can maintain an "I can do it" or "I can get through it" type of attitude. People with high self-esteem live by Reverend Robert Schuller's words, "Tough times never last, but tough people do."

You are more motivated and ambitious. People with high self-esteem tend to set more goals and seem to accomplish more with their lives. These same people have the feeling that they make a difference in their world. Whether it be their work environment, their families, or their civic accomplishments, people with high self-esteem know they make a positive difference.

You will have better relationships. When you have high self-esteem, you tend to treat others better. You can do this easily because you feel good about yourself. When you treat others better, they will treat you better in return. When you have high self-esteem, it dictates what relationships you will even enter into. If you are treated poorly by someone, your self-esteem thermostat will tell you that you deserve to be treated better and you will look elsewhere for your rewards.

You will live life more humorously. Have you ever had an incident in your life that devastated you? Maybe it was a relationship that soured, an embarrassing situation, or a task that you did not perform as well as you would have liked. Usually, when one of these situations occurs, we feel terrible. We feel like we failed! Then, as time passes, we slowly start to see the situation as humorous. In fact, years later, we can sit around the dinner table and share the entire incident in the form of a joke. The benefit of having high self-esteem is that you have the ability to see the humor sooner.

You will be more open to change and risk-taking. Whether it is new ideas, situations, opportunities, or challenges, high self-esteem makes you more willing to experience new things. Anything new requires learning. Along with learning comes mistakes. People with high self-esteem look at mistakes as learning and use this learning to grow. Sir Thomas Watson of IBM once said, "If you want to succeed, double your failure rate!"

You will be more open to criticism. Supervisors with low self-esteem do not have the ability to listen or accept feedback from their employees. When you have high self-esteem, you will find it easier to accept feedback from others. You recognize their responses as a learning experience and incorporate what you learn to make yourself a better person. People with low self-esteem spend their time defending their actions, blaming others, and making excuses about why things have to be the way they are.

You will be better able to think for yourself. Supervisors with high self-esteem are able to accept the opinions of others, assimilate the information, and form their own definite feelings, opinions, and positions. With high self-esteem, you have a strong sense of what is right and wrong and that makes your decision making an easier process. With strong self-esteem, you will find it easier to be more assertive and stick up for what you believe is right.

You will have the ability to accept people, including yourself, as they are, not as you would like them to be. When you have high self-esteem, you have the ability to walk in the other person's moccasins. With high self-esteem, you will not feel a strong need to change your life for another person's approval. You will also be less inclined to try to change others.

Fifteen Steps to Higher Self-Esteem

In the preceding pages, we learned about self-esteem—what it is and the benefits of obtaining high self-esteem. Now let's look at what we can do to raise our self-esteem. There are hundreds of little things you can do on a daily basis that will enhance your self-esteem.

Here are 15 of the things we feel are most important for supervisors.

1. **Live for today**. One phrase we'd like to cut from the English language is "if only." "If only" I would get one more promotion, could make a certain income, close a certain sale; "if only"

19

I could afford a bigger house or a fancier car; "if only" my boss would get off my back; "if only" I could motivate this one employee...then I would really be happy. Focus on what is good right now. Each day ask yourself, "What is going well right now?" and "What can I do today for myself?"

2. **Set goals.** In order to gain mastery over your environment, it is important that you be able to accomplish the things in life that you feel are important. Setting and achieving predetermined goals is one of the most important roads to travel if you are going to increase your self-esteem. When you set goals, you will realize you do have control in your life, you will be more motivated, and you will be proud of your accomplishments. (Information on goal setting is provided in Chapter 14.)

3. **Associate with others who have high self-esteem.** You will encounter negative people who will always point out the negative in any situation. Some will even purposely try to drag you down. When you associate with other individuals who have high self-esteem, you will reap the benefits they have to offer. They tend to be happier with life, deal easier with change and adversity, and will offer you support and unequaled encouragement. Choose your friends and associates wisely.

4. **Dress and look your best always.** You can tell a lot about how a person feels by looking at the way he or she dresses. People respond to us, in part, by our appearance. By feeling good about your appearance, you send a message to others that you care for and like yourself. The response from others will reinforce these feelings. How you look on the outside deeply affects how you feel on the inside.

5. **Set your own standards.** By setting internal standards, you will be comparing you to you. This means we have to believe in our own uniqueness. When we appreciate the true nature of self-esteem, we see that it is not competitive or comparative. Genuine self-esteem is not expressed by being better than others or diminishing others so we can elevate ourselves. It is developed by setting personal goals, challenging ourselves, and feeling proud of our accomplishments. You decide what standards are important to you.

6. **Look people in the eye.** Before you can look others in the eye, you need to be able to look yourself in the eye. When you look into a mirror, you need to feel good about you. Most people will tell you that they like people better who are able to look them eyeball-to-eyeball. Research has shown that people who look others in the eye are perceived as more honest, trustworthy, and credible. Those three qualities are valuable to anyone.

7. **Volunteer your name first.** Whether you are
    introducing yourself or answering the
    telephone, you tell a lot about yourself by
    volunteering your name first in a conversation.
    You are telling others you have self-
    confidence, self-respect, and are proud of who
    you are. Others, in turn, will respond to you
    with a higher level of respect.

8. **Treat everyone you meet with dignity and
    respect.** From the president of your
    corporation to the janitor who cleans your
    office, from your significant other to the person
    who waits on your table when you eat out—
    treat everyone with dignity and respect. With
    this attitude, people will go out of their way to
    help you. Friendships are easier to attain and
    you will find most people will like you better.
    As a side benefit, you will never have to worry
    about offending the wrong person. Being liked
    by others once again enhances our self-
    esteem.

9. **Improve your communication skills.**
    Communication is the tool that connects us to
    others. Clearly expressing your ideas allows
    you to be understood. Listening allows you to
    grow, learn, and open up to other people and
    ideas. Communication is the glue that binds
    friendships, marriages, and successful
    relationships at work. There are hundreds of
    ways available to improve your communication
    skills: books, tapes, seminars, Toastmasters,
    etc. Find one and take some time to improve

your ability to connect with others. You will see that as your confidence in your communication skills improves, so will your self-esteem.

10. **Remember, all successful people have experienced failure.** Most people who have accomplished anything great have experienced many failures. The difference is that these successful people view failure differently than most. They use the failure as a learning experience and benefit from it. Dr. Warren Bennis, in his book *Leaders, The Strategies for Taking Charge*, describes how all the great leaders he interviewed had at least one devastating experience in their life. Gail Sheehy, in her book *Pathfinders*, describes the same phenomena. The difference with the people these two authors describe is the way they viewed the failure in their lives: They viewed it as a learning experience.

11. **Develop the habit of positive self-talk.** Your self-esteem is shaped by the way you communicate with yourself. The sooner you can change the way you communicate with yourself, the sooner your communication with others will change as well. When you change your communication with others, it changes the way others respond to you and this reinforces your positive self-talk. As your self-talk is enhanced and becomes more positive, your self-esteem will follow in a positive manner. Assess your self-talk. Are you being

kind to yourself? If you don't like what you hear, change your negative self-talk into positive self-talk. Focus on positive belief in yourself.

12. **Be a volunteer or a mentor.** Give back. Help others as you have been helped. Give some of your time to those who could benefit from your friendship or expertise. Whether it is a person or an organization, you will feel good after you have touched another in a positive way. It usually costs you very little and you have a lot to gain knowing you have helped someone.

13. **Try it until you make it!** Many people ask, "How can I exhibit the behaviors of a person with high self-esteem when I do not feel that way?" Unfortunately, many do not realize that behaviors that generate good self-esteem are also expressions of good self-esteem. Even when you do not feel like manifesting high self-esteem behaviors, TRY IT! If you act like you have high self-esteem, high self-esteem will follow. The only secret to enhancing and maintaining high self-esteem is to practice, practice, and practice some more.

14. **Focus on what you want, not what you do not want.** People with high self-esteem focus on what they want in life, not what they do not want or what they want to avoid. If you want a new job, an improved relationship, or a slimmer you, do not focus on being stuck where you are, the negative aspects of the

relationship, or your current weight. Put your sights on the new job: What will it be? Where will it be? What will you be doing? Focus on how the relationship will be better: Is there better communication? Do we have greater mutual respect? Are we having more fun? Imagine the slimmer you: How will you feel? What will you look like? How will others react to you? Remember, you will get what you expect. So expect the best.

15. **Take full responsibility for your life.** Men and women who enjoy high self-esteem have an active orientation to life rather than a passive one. They take full responsibility for the attainment of their goals. They ask the questions, "Where do I want to be?" and "How do I get there?" They do not wait for others to fulfill their wants and dreams. Self-responsibility is indispensable to good self-esteem. Avoiding self-responsibility victimizes us in our own lives. It leaves us helpless. We give power to everyone except ourselves. When we are frustrated, we look for someone to blame, finding others at fault for our unhappiness. In contrast, the appreciation of self-responsibility can be an exhilarating and empowering experience. It places our lives back into our own hands. In short, people with high self-esteem take responsibility for their own existence.

Tips for Success:
Confidence and Self-Esteem

1. Recognize that your self-esteem and self-image impact every aspect of your role as a supervisor.

2. Stop valuing your self-worth by comparing yourself to others. Set your own standards and then strive to achieve those standards.

3. Set realistic and obtainable goals. It is the fastest way to raise your self-esteem. When you set a goal and achieve it, you feel you have mastery over your environment.

4. Associate with high self-esteemers. You do have a choice as to whom you associate with. Individuals with high self-esteem have the capacity to help build your self-esteem.

5. Laugh sooner. If you have ever experienced a crisis or a failure, you know at some point you are able to laugh about it. The goal is to laugh sooner.

6. Give and accept compliments. When you give sincere compliments, people like you better. When you accept compliments, it demonstrates high self-esteem.

7. Ask for and accept feedback from others. When people care about you enough to offer feedback, either positive or negative, you have the opportunity to grow.

8. Take full responsibility for your actions. Empowered people with high self-esteem know they are responsible for their decisions and actions.

9. Use positive self-talk, because what you think about comes about.

10. Remember, successful people have experienced failure. Successful people with high self-esteem do not view failure as failure, but rather as an opportunity to learn how to do things differently.

27

Leading Organizational Change

*"The trouble with the future is that it usually arrives
before we're ready for it."*
Arnold H. Glasow

Being a leader in an organization during the
turbulent past decade has been challenging, and at
times, perhaps has seemed like an overwhelming
task. All indicators are that organizations will
continue facing challenges created by sharp
economic swings, keen competitive pressures,
globalization of the marketplace, and reshaping of
businesses worldwide. Simply put, change is here
to stay.

Whether we like it or not, organizational changes
result in supervisors having to implement those
changes. Having an understanding of the way
change affects our organization, and recognizing
the resulting impact of the change on the
individuals within our organization, is critical.

Unfortunately for managers and supervisors, it's a
given fact that employees do not all respond to
change with the attitude, "Fantastic, another
organizational change and I'm excited to be a part

of it!" We have found that when change is introduced to an organization, or better yet, rumored, employees often resist change in a variety of ways.

Reasons People Resist Change

The following ten reasons best describe some typical reasons why some employees have a tough time changing their mindsets and behavior:

1. **Fear of failure.** Some employee resistance to change is rooted in fear. During periods of change, an employee may feel the need to cling to the past because it was a more secure, predictable time.

2. **Creatures of habit.** Doing things in the same routine, predictable manner is comfortable. Asking people to change the way they operate or think requires them to move outside their comfort zone. "We've always done it this way, so why do we need to change?" becomes the rallying cry for people who have difficulty changing their routines.

3. **No obvious need.** "If it has been working all this time, and working well, why do we need to change?" Like the old expression, "If it ain't broke, why fix it?", employees within an organization may only see a change from the perspective of the impact it has on them and their particular jobs.

4. **Loss of control.** Employees working in familiar routines develop a sense of control over their work environment. They know what works and what doesn't. Therefore, they are confident about their contribution to the organization. For some employees, asking them to change the way they operate creates a feeling of being powerless and confused during the transition.

5. **Concern about support system.** Employees operating within predictable routines know their support system will back them up during challenging times. When organizational systems and structures are changed, some employees may resist the change because they lack confidence in their support system.

6. **Closed mind.** For a variety of reasons, some employees seem to approach all change from an attitude of "Please don't confuse me with any further facts or supporting documentation about this proposed or required change—I've already made up my mind!"

7. **Unwilling to learn.** Some employees, hesitant about trying new routines, express their resistance by being unwilling to learn anything new. They may say, "I already know all that I need to know," or "I don't need to know that!"

8. **Fear that the change may not be better.** If things have been going well, some employees resist change because they fear that the

change will not result in improvement.
Focusing only on their part of the operation,
they may fail to realize that change is needed
in order for the organization to stay
competitive.

9. **Fear of the unknown.** Employees may resist a
change within their organization because it is
something unfamiliar. Not knowing much
about the specifics of the change, they think
about a worst case scenario, which can be very
scary. Rather than find out more, they let fear
of the unknown become their rationale for not
giving the change a chance.

10. **Fear of personal impact.** Viewing change
from a personal standpoint, some employees
may respond by asking how the change will
benefit them directly. Will it make their job
easier? Will they have to work harder? Will the
change put their job security in jeopardy? Will
the change force them to work with different
people or learn a new job? These are all initial
responses supervisors may experience when
they announce an organizational change to
employees.

Typical Employee Responses Regarding Change

During times of organization change, you will
notice employees reacting to change with a variety
of responses. As a leader tasked with implementing
organization change, it is important for a
supervisor to be able to understand typical

32

employee reactions. The following reactions are some typical responses to organizational change:

1. **Not me!** Typically, when employees are asked to do a different job, or change the way they currently do a particular job, they respond in denial with, "Not me!" They may begin to tell their supervisor about someone else better suited for the job or deny that they are capable of making the proposed change.

2. **What will this do to my job security?** "What's in it for me?" is often an employee's first response upon learning about a proposed organizational change. It is natural for employees to see change in perspective to their own job security.

3. **Anger.** Some employees are so resistant to change that they become frustrated and angry. Their anger may be repressed, causing an increased stress level, or overt, resulting in emotional outbursts. Whether repressed or overt, anger is a typical reaction to change.

4. **Gossip.** Gossip, always an organizational challenge, often escalates during periods of organizational change. Employees who respond to organizational change with frustration, anger, and disbelief often resort to vicious gossip or "back-stabbing" activities.

5. **Who's in charge here?** During times when organizations are restructuring, it is natural

33

for employees to question leadership. If employees are concerned that they will be working for a new supervisor, there will undoubtedly be unrest during the transition period as they anticipate changing allegiance from one leader to another.

6. **Panic!** Some employees, finding comfort in a predictable routine, panic at the mere mention of change. For them, upsetting the routine and making changes in the way they normally proceed with their jobs can cause panic.

7. **I quit!** Some employees may actually be so resistant to accepting organizational changes that they elect to quit rather than make the needed changes. Electing to stand on one's principles and fight change by quitting often makes the point, but usually at a cost to the employee making the point, not to the organization.

8. **This is a challenge!** Employees viewing change as a challenge feel they can rise to the occasion. They feel that they have what it takes to be a contributing team player when the change affects their work world. They remain open to new ideas, ask questions, and feel confident in their ability to acquire the knowledge needed to complete the task. They exhibit a "can do" attitude in their approach to change.

9. **Maybe I could adjust to this change.** Some employees don't embrace change enthusiastically or jump out of their seats ready to accept a challenge resulting from organizational change. Instead, they may watch from the sidelines, but they remain open-minded. They may not commit initially, but after a period of observation, agree to remain open and give the change a chance.

10. **Enthusiasm.** Some employees naturally approach life and challenges more enthusiastically than others. These employees have the gift of embracing change enthusiastically. Instead of trying to pick apart proposed changes and find all the ways they won't work, enthusiastic employees see change as a natural part of an organization's evolution. These are employees who understand the bigger picture. They understand the value in making change.

Employees will exhibit a variety of responses to change. Fortunately, there are several specific actions and straightforward approaches managers and supervisors can take to help guide their employees successfully through organizational change. These guidelines can make times of change some of the most rewarding and productive times in your leadership history!

Guidelines for Organizational Change

1. **Involve employees in the change process.**
   We are firm believers that employees are not
   so much against change as they are against
   being changed. The sooner you involve
   employees in the process, the better off you
   will be implementing the change. A formal
   communication channel will be more effective
   at implementing change than a negative
   informal one consisting of rumors and gossip.
   Involving employees helps employees move
   from a "Not me!" response to a greater
   understanding of why the change is needed.

2. **Interview employees.** It is critical that
   managers and supervisors understand what
   employees are feeling regarding the change. It
   is only when you accurately understand their
   feelings that you know what issues need to be
   addressed. Implementing change requires the
   ability to sell. It is difficult to sell effectively
   without understanding your buyer's needs,
   concerns, and fears.

3. **Ask questions, don't tell.** We are fond of the
   statement, "You can tell tough employees, but
   you can't tell them much." People who do not
   deal well with change generally are the same
   employees who cannot be "told" anything. For
   this reason, we recommend asking them
   questions rather than telling them why the
   changes are taking place. Asking rather than
   telling helps reduce feelings of anxiety or anger

that the employee may be experiencing related to the change.

4. **Get both negative and positive informal leaders involved.** Most managers and supervisors get the positive informal leaders involved in helping implement changes. They have a reputation for supporting management, regardless of the change. The mistake many managers make is not getting the negative informal leaders involved in the beginning stages of the change process. By involving them, you know what their objections and concerns are regarding the change. Knowing their concerns will help you design your change strategy.

5. **Don't cover all the bases yourself.** Too often managers and supervisors feel they must use self-protective measures, especially during organizational change. They start by trying to police all activities. You should concentrate on effective delegation during the early stages of the change process. Effective delegation is particularly good for two reasons. First, it helps you manage and maintain your workload. Second, it gives your employees a sense of involvement. That positions them to share in the responsibility for change.

6. **Raise expectations.** Now, more than ever, you should ask more from your employees. It is expected that more work needs to be done during the change process. While it may be

more practical to expect less in terms of performance, this is the time to raise your levels of performance for both yourself and your employees. Require performance improvements and make the process challenging, but remember to keep goals realistic so you eliminate frustration and failure.

7. **Ask employees for their commitment.** Once the change has been announced, it is important that you personally ask for each employee's commitment to implement the change successfully. It is equally important that you tell the employee that if there are problems, you want to hear about them. Remember, if a negative employee does not tell you about problems, you can be sure he will be telling other employees about why the change will not work.

8. **Overcommunicate.** The change process usually means that normal communication channels in the organization won't be working as well as they usually do. During this time, your employees will be hungrier than ever for information and answers. You can "beef up" communication in two ways. First, give employees an opportunity to give you input. Start by becoming more available and asking more questions. Get employee opinions and reactions to the changes. Second, strive to be specific. Clear up rumors and misinformation that clutter the communication changes.

Remember, it is almost impossible to overcommunicate.

9. **Be firm, but flexible.** As you introduce a change, it is important that you see the change through to completion. Abandoning it halfway through the change destroys your credibility. Remain committed to the success of the change effort, but flexible because you may have to adapt to a myriad of situations to successfully implement your change.

10. **Keep positive.** Your attitude as a manager or supervisor will be a major factor in determining what type of climate is exhibited by your employees. Your attitude is the one thing that keeps you in control. Change can be stressful and confusing. Try to remain upbeat, positive, and enthusiastic. Foster motivation in others. During times of transition and change, make a commitment to acknowledge your employees for their extra effort.

Finally, the best way to predict the future is to invent it. Consider what changes are coming, what needs to happen, and how you can contribute! Instead of changing with the times, make it a habit to change, just a little ahead of the times.

Tips for Success:
Organizational Change

1. Be a role model for leading the new change. Gain a reputation for leading your team forward, not defending the past.

2. Hold yourself accountable for successful implementation of change. Maintain high personal standards and hold others accountable to agreed-upon team standards.

3. Develop a compelling positive vision of the future. While you may not have all the details, the more positive your vision, the greater the chance for your success. Also, the clearer your vision, the easier it is for your employees to follow your lead.

4. Set clear, specific goals and communicate the goals to each member on your team so they know the target and understand how their individual effort contributes to the team's success.

5. Double your communication efforts during periods of rapid organizational change. Overcommunicate to make sure that employees feel they are getting enough communication regarding the change.

6. During times of change, focus on ensuring customer satisfaction, both internally and externally. This focus reminds all members of the team of your real purpose for existence.

7. Show unwavering commitment to the success of your team and your organization. Expect the waters to get choppy during times of fast change. Hang on. Ride the waves. Your tenacity will be a source of inspiration for your team.

8. Get in the habit of rewarding the messenger, even if the news is not good. During times of change, you want to know, firsthand, what your employees are thinking and feeling. Their insights will help make you a more informed, better decision maker.

9. Expect resistance. Robert F. Kennedy said, "Twenty percent of the people are against any change!"

10. Don't drag your heels and resist change. Move fast! All the research shows that fast change is easier to deal with than slow change.

4

Managing Time to Accomplish Your Goals

"The only way there is true equality in this world is that we all have the same amount of time. Some people just accomplish more."

Peter B. Stark

I just don't have the time. How many times have you heard this comment? How many times have you used it yourself? Every time we do not accomplish something we should have, or intended to, this line seems to surface. Many managers and supervisors frequently feel the pressure of a lack of time. They literally run out of time. The reasons? Lack of priorities, unclear goals, interruptions, unproductive meetings, disorganization, inability to say "no," and possibly ineffective delegation.

The 168 Hour Limit

There are two facts we know about time. First, there are exactly 24 hours or 1,440 minutes in every day. That amounts to 168 hours in a week and 8,760 hours in a year. Second, we all have the same amount of time. So the question is not one of where do you find more time. You cannot do it. The real question we need to be asking is how do we manage the things that we do in the 168 hours that are available in the week.

The following is a typical breakdown of how activities may consume our time:

Time at work (9 hours per day)	45
Travel to work (1 hour per day)	5
Eating meals (2 hours per day)	14
Sleeping (7 hours per day)	49
Bathing and dressing (1 hour per day)	<u>7</u>
Total	120

What this means is that we have 48 hours to spend on other activities. Things such as:

Family time	____
Leisure activities	____
Religious/spiritual worship	____
Paying bills	____
Personal growth	____
Activities for children	____
Grocery shopping	____
Yard work	____
Cleaning the house	____
Maintaining the car	____
Watching television	____
Reading the newspaper	____
Free time	____

If the typical breakdown of activities is fairly accurate for you, then you have approximately 48 hours to spend on other activities. If you have a career that takes more time, say 55 hours in a week, then you only have 38 hours to divide up on other activities. If you have a new baby or very young children in your family, you may have even fewer hours for other activities.

Conducting a Time Management Audit

If you are going to be successful managing your time, then it is critical that you know how you spend your time. If we are focusing on accomplishment, then it is important you realize when you are productive and when you are not. The best way to conduct a time audit is to record your time, activity by activity, as you progress throughout the day. To conduct a time audit, follow the seven steps listed below:

1.   List boundary times. For example, list what time you get up in the morning and what time you go to bed at night.

2.   Then write down/fill in activities that are conducted on a ritual basis: things like taking a shower, reading the paper, driving to work and back, or eating meals are things that you do on a consistent daily basis.

3.   Shade in meetings and other large blocks of time where you spent your day.

4.   Outline all other activities that made up your day.

5. Compute the length of time you spent in that activity.

6. Circle anything you accomplished or completed.

7. Summarize the areas where you did not make the best possible use of your time.

One problem with this method of a time audit is that when you forget to record your activities as you complete them, you may find you have blank spots during your day. If someone asked you what you did at that time slot, you may find it necessary to reply, "I worked...I think."

A sample time audit might look something like this:

5:00	am	Get up and fix the coffee	10 minutes
5:10	am	Take a shower, get dressed	30 minutes
5:40	am	Read newspaper	15 minutes
5:55	am	Organize day (home office)	30 minutes
6:25	am	Fix breakfast for family	35 minutes
7:00	am	Help get children ready for school	30 minutes
7:30	am	Take children to school	20 minutes
7:50	am	Drive to office	10 minutes
8:00	am	Staff meeting	1 hour
9:00	am	Return phone calls	15 minutes
9:15	am	Write article for company newsletter	30 minutes
9:45	am	Listen to John whine about the policy change	30 minutes

10:15	am	Solve a problem for an angry customer	10 minutes
10:25	am	Leave for a 10:30 meeting	5 minutes
10:30	am	Attend meeting on the XYZ project	2 hours
12:30	pm	Lunch	45 minutes
1:15	pm	Return phone calls	15 minutes
1:30	pm	Update boss (unexpected)	1 hour
2:30	pm	Handle a customer problem	10 minutes
2:40	pm	Write a proposal for the ABC Company	1 hour
3:40	pm	Take care of three phone calls	15 minutes
3:55	pm	John back for clarification...more whining	10 minutes
4:05	pm	Work on Mary's performance review (overdue)	25 minutes
4:30	pm	Walk to Andy's desk to update the ABC project	15 minutes
4:45	pm	Return two phone calls	10 minutes
4:55	pm	Talk with Larry about football game (unexpected)	15 minutes
5:10	pm	Organize desk	10 minutes
5:20	pm	Leave to pick up children from day care	30 minutes
5:50	pm	Get home, decide what to have for dinner	15 minutes
6:05	pm	Prepare and eat dinner	55 minutes
7:00	pm	Clean up after dinner	15 minutes
7:15	pm	Help children with homework	45 minutes
8:00	pm	Watch television with family	30 minutes
8:30	pm	Get children ready for bed	30 minutes

9:00	pm	Decide to watch TV but fall asleep	2 hours
11:00	pm	Wake up and go to bed	6 hours
5:00	am	Get up and start the routine all over again	

What are the benefits of conducting a time audit?
It lets you see how you really do spend your time.
Some of the learning points from this audit are:

> I spent four hours in meetings in the day.
> I spent 40 minutes of my day listening to John
> whine.
> I wasted 15 minutes walking to Andy's desk
> when inter-office mail would have worked
> just fine.
> Mary's review was the most important task I
> had to complete and I still did not get it
> done.
> The ABC proposal could have been easily
> delegated if I had planned ahead.

A blank page is provided so you can complete a
time audit. You are welcome to make multiple
copies if you would like to chart more than one
day. We recommend that you conduct a time audit
at least four times a year.

Daily Time Log

Note: Do not try to account for each minute of the day.
Account for 15-minute blocks of time.

Day of Week: M T W T F Date:			
Time	Activity	Time	Activity
6:00		1:00	
6:15		1:15	
6:30		1:30	
6:45		1:45	
7:00		2:00	
7:15		2:15	
7:30		2:30	
7:45		2:45	
8:00		3:00	
8:15		3:15	
8:30		3:30	
8:45		3:45	
9:00		4:00	
9:15		4:15	
9:30		4:30	
9:45		4:45	
10:00		5:00	
10:15		5:15	
10:30		5:30	
10:45		5:45	
11:00		6:00	
11:15		6:15	
11:30		6:30	
11:45		6:45	
12:00		7:00	
12:15		7:15	
12:30		7:30	
12:45		7:45	
Was this day: ___Typical? ___More busy? ___Less busy? Comments:			

Successful Time Management and Task Accomplishment

You will find the following four steps helpful in managing your time.

Step One: Create a Master "To Do" List

This is a critical step. Many managers and supervisors try to keep track of all their tasks by leaving reminder notes for themselves. Yes, 3M Post-it notes work great for reminders. Little slips of paper and telephone message slips are other great reminders. The problem with this method is that little pieces of paper get lost. It can also be confusing. So, take all your tasks and record them on one "master" piece of paper. There are several excellent organizer programs available for use on your computer which make the task even easier. This first step is critical in helping you get organized.

Step Two: Prioritize Your Tasks

One thing is certain. Despite what many managers think, you can only do one task at a time. And, we need to do the most important task first. The following five categories may be helpful in breaking down your priorities:

Category A—Highest priority (critical to my success and urgent). Category A tasks are easy to distinguish. If you do not get them done, bad things may happen. Whether it is your boss, employee, or a client, if you do not get these tasks completed, the person who needed the task accomplished would lower your performance rating if he or she were to give you one. Many supervisors and managers have lost their jobs or customers because they did not recognize a task as Category A.

Category B—Proactive (helpful to my success but not urgent). A great example of a Category B task would be going to a time management seminar. It is not critical that you go right at this moment. But, by going, you may find better ways to manage your time. By managing your time better, you accomplish more. By using some time each day for Category B tasks, you will eliminate some of the fires that come up on a daily basis. Thus, you will have more time for your Category A tasks.

Category C—Routine ordinary tasks (time discretionary and time bound). These are tasks that need to be completed on a routine basis. A report is a great example. It has a specific date and time when it is due. You could work on the report at night after dinner. You could do it first thing in the morning. It is your discretion when you complete the report. The only time the report becomes a Category A task is 15 minutes before it is due.

Category D—Routine ordinary tasks (not time bound). These are the tasks and projects that you would like to complete, but there are no penalties or time constraints if you do not. A great example is that many of us have a stack of papers or other documents on our desk. Sometimes it is a big stack; other times it is a small stack. With D's, you can almost always delegate or dump. If it has been in your D pile for a month, it will not make much difference who does it or if it gets done at all.

Category E—Leisure time. Everyone needs to spend some time each day or week doing something that is leisurable or pleasurable to you. Leisure is different things to different people. For some people, going to the beach and enjoying the sunshine is leisure. For others, this same activity is stressful. Pick what works best for you and spend some time each week or each day in a leisure activity.

Step Three: Sub-Categorize Your Priorities

Once you have determined which tasks are your Category A priorities, then the next step is to determine which is the highest priority, most urgent item of the A's. Label that task A1. Then take the second highest priority Category A and label that A2. Do the same for the rest of the Category A's, B's, C's, and D's. An example of how this prioritization may look follows:

A1   Complete Mary's review
A2   Complete the proposal to the Henley
        Company

A3 Return phone calls
B1 Hold a staff meeting
B2 Clean off my desk
C1 Prepare budget comparison (due in two weeks)
C2 Return call to Larry
D1 Go through the stack of junk on my credenza
D2 Read old magazines

Four Tips to Help You Maintain Your Priorities

1. **Do your A's first.** Many supervisors find it a lot easier to do C's. The classic line is, "I will get these C's off the list first and then I will get to the A's." The problem is you run out of time before you get to complete your A's. C's will not cost you your job. A's will, so do them first.

2. **Work on your B's each day.** The easiest thing to do is to say you never have any time to move your B's up on your list. An example of a B might be to create a model or template for one of the types of projects you are required to complete. If you had the model or template, others in the department could complete the task for you. Commit to making time each day to work on a B.

3. **Place less emphasis on C's.** Unfortunately, C's are usually easier to complete than A's. For this reason, the natural tendency is to do C's first. This is an error that many supervisors and managers make. We say to ourselves, "I

will just get these few things out of the way, then I will complete the tough task." Each day, it is important to consciously prioritize each task. Returning an angry customer's phone call (an A) needs to take precedence over reviewing your monthly budget (a C). Once our tasks our prioritized, we need to do the highest priority, most urgent item first.

4. **Use the GUTS theory on D's.** Everyone has a few D's. The best example is the pile of things you have stacked up in places like your desk, credenza, or some other slightly out-of-the-way location. With D's, you can practice the GUTS theory. GUTS stands for:

    G = Give it away to someone else
    U = Use it
    T = Throw it away
    S = Save and file it

    If you will practice the GUTS theory, you will eliminate a lot of clutter from your life. The problem with unattended D's is that they eventually multiply and will psychologically overwhelm you. Every time you walk into your office and see your stack of D's or a cluttered drawer or shelf, it bothers you because you are reminded of what you have not done. Use GUTS and you will keep your D's to a manageable level.

Step Four: Identify Your Time Wasters

What wastes your time? The following are a list of typical time wasters. Place a check by the ones you feel have the biggest impact in wasting your time.

___ Socializing	___ Opening junk mail
___ Misplacing something	___ Unclear directions from boss
___ Watching television	___ Procrastination
___ Paperwork	___ Tough employees
___ Correcting others' mistakes	___ Unproductive meetings
___ Fighting fires	___ Interruptions
___ Traffic to/from work	___ _____
___ _____	___ _____

Once you know where you waste your time, following the suggestions in this chapter will help you overcome these time wasters and make the best possible use of your time.

Tips for Success:
Time Management

1. Organize your work environment. Does the environment you work in work for you or against you? The more your environment is organized, the more productive you will be.

2. Establish place habits. It is estimated that the average American spends six months of his or her life looking for items that are lost, misplaced, or just plain missing. Think how

much time you could save if everything you needed had a specific place, just like your screwdriver or flashlight.

3. Create a master daily "To Do" list. Each day you need to create a new "To Do" list. The tasks may take longer than you like, but if each task is on your list, it will eventually be done. (There are several types of computer-generated organizers people utilize that do an excellent job.)

4. Prioritize your tasks. Once you have prioritized your tasks, do your highest rated, most urgent items first.

5. Set goals. Without a specific set of goals, it really does not matter how you spend your time. (Information about setting goals is included in Chapter 14.)

6. Cluster common tasks. When you return to your office after a meeting, there will be several phone messages on your voice mail. You can quickly cluster the messages and return them within five minutes. Clustering common tasks saves time.

7. Delineate time blocks. Block off a portion of time and work on only that task during the specified time frame. This technique works great when you have been procrastinating.

8. Stop procrastinating. Make a list of all the things in your life that you have been postponing. Then set a goal with a specific plan and time frame to accomplish those procrastinated tasks.

9. Delegate where appropriate. It is often more appropriate and efficient for someone else to accomplish the task. (For more information on effective delegation, refer to Chapter 6.)

10. Take the one-minute acid test. Ask, "Is what I am doing right now the best possible and most important use of my time?" Also ask, "Five years from now, what will be the most important task to have completed, task A or task B?" These questions also help you put things in proper perspective.

Communicating Effectively

*"I know you believe you understood what you think
I said, but I'm not sure you realize that what you
heard is not what I meant to say."*
Sign on an executive's desk

Communication is one of the most challenging
aspects of supervision. When employees are asked
to describe their best and worst bosses, guess what
item is at the top of both lists? You guessed it—
communication!

The most common items that describe both the
best bosses and the worst bosses are listed below.

Description of Bosses

Worst Boss	Best Boss
Doesn't care about others	Gives feedback
Poor communicator	Good communicator
Doesn't listen	Listens
Gives mixed messages	Speaks clearly
Demands instead of asks	Solicits input
Self-focused	Other-focused

Research has consistently shown that
communication ability is the characteristic judged
by supervisors and managers to be most critical in

determining promotability. A manager's number one challenge can be summed up in one word: communication.

What We Know about Communication

There are certain aspects of communication that impact our day-to-day lives.

1. **No matter how hard one tries, one cannot avoid communicating.** Many times we think we are not communicating because we are not verbally communicating. That is simply not the case. We are always communicating, whether we want to or not. We communicate nonverbally—with our eyes, facial expressions, gestures—and even by the color of our skin. During 30 minutes of discussion, people can exchange approximately 800 different nonverbal messages. The messages we send without words have a greater impact than when we speak.

2. **Communicating does not necessarily mean understanding.** Can you think of a time when you were convinced that you got your message across but later found out quite the opposite?

3. **Communication is irreversible.** Once you have communicated a message and it has been received, either verbally or nonverbally, it is irreversible. Have you ever said something that you have regretted? Or, have you ever wished you had said something and did not?

4. **Communication is affected by physical and social settings.** When we interact with someone, it is not in isolation but within a specific physical and social surrounding. For example, when our boss talks to us about a memo from behind his or her desk, the conversation will probably be quite different than when we are having lunch at the corner deli.

5. **Communication is dynamic.** Communication is an ongoing and ever-changing process. As participants in communication, we are constantly affected by other people's messages and, as a consequence, we undergo continual change. Every time we interact with someone, we leave that moment with new information...and a changed relationship.

Making Communication Work

All critical management skills require effective communication. Whether you are leading, coaching, delegating, building a team, making decisions, counseling, hiring, or just about any management activity you can think of, you will need to communicate. The following valuable communication tips related to speaking and listening will help you improve your ability to communicate effectively.

Speak Clearly

As a manager, one of your primary responsibilities is to get the right message to the right person, to

get the results you expect. Because the
communication process is so complex, getting your
message across is not an easy task. Barriers or
roadblocks can get in the way: lack of
understanding (on your part or theirs),
interruptions, noise, emotional state (yours or
theirs), bias, prejudice, boredom, resentment,
language problems, culture, physical environment,
lack of trust, poor listening habits, mixed
messages, and unclear priorities.

To work your way around these barriers, consider
the following ideas:

1. **Think through what you want to say before
   you say it.** Begin by focusing on your
   intention or goal. Be clear about what you
   expect as a result of your communication. Do
   you want an employee to do a certain job? Do
   you want a co-worker to support you on a
   particular project? Do you want your boss to
   give you more information? In your mind,
   clearly define what you want to accomplish.
   Once you are clear about what your
   communication goal is, you can focus on the
   message you need to get across.

2. **Once you have made your point, ask each
   listener for feedback.** Make sure that each
   listener has understood your intention and
   specifically what it is you want. You can get
   this feedback by observing and asking.
   Observe the listener's behavior. Is it in
   agreement? Does he or she appear to have

questions or to disagree? Also pay attention to the nonverbal cues you are receiving.

3. **Speak clearly and concisely.** Some people believe that wordiness is a sign of knowledge or power, but it actually gets in the way of effective communication. Being overly verbose is a distraction. Many people will simply tune out a speaker who is too wordy. Keep your words and sentences short and to the point.

4. **Speak with enthusiasm and expressiveness.** If you are trying to convince others or to motivate a team or individual, your ability to be enthusiastic is critical. Be aware of your tone of voice. Are you speaking in a monotone? If so, this is one of the quickest ways to lose the listener. Add variety to your voice by varying your rate of speech and tone of voice. Adding examples, personal stories or experiences, and analogies or metaphors always make a speaker more interesting.

5. **Develop a natural and informal style.** People are more likely to listen if you appear natural and informal in your discussions. Many employees complain that their bosses are stiff or formal when communicating with them. If you want to open up communication, be yourself. Speak with your employees as you would to a friend. This informal approach will help you to build trust and credibility with others.

6. **Be sincere.** Your employees, co-workers, and your boss can see right through you! It is important to always be sincere in your communication. This includes letting others know when you are unsure or do not understand. It also includes telling the truth and being as direct and honest as you can be. When others truly believe that you speak from the heart, you are beginning to create a trusting relationship. Others will be honest with you in return. When people on your team are open and honest with one another, the chances of getting and receiving clear communication will increase ten-fold.

Listening for Understanding

Communication is a two-way street. In addition to speaking clearly, the effective communicator is a good listener. Listening involves not only hearing the speaker's words, but also understanding the message and its importance to the speaker.

Listening is one of a supervisor's biggest challenges, impacted by many factors. To overcome barriers to effective listening, try some of the following tips for improving your listening ability:

1. **Develop an attitude of wanting to listen.** Being a good listener starts with a positive attitude toward listening. Even if you do not feel like listening, remember that you can always learn something from everyone and that listening is a critical component to establishing trusting relationships. Good

leaders always want to listen because they know the value of continuous learning. They also know that you cannot continue to learn if you do not listen.

2. **Focus your attention on understanding the other person's meaning, not on formulating your response.** A good listener is "other-focused" rather than "self-focused." Your goal is to understand the other person. To do this, give your undivided attention, ask questions for clarification, and check your perceptions for understanding. Focusing your attention on the speaker will also help you to listen without interrupting.

3. **Show the speaker that you are listening.** A critical part of the listening process is letting the speaker know that you are interested in his or her message. Ways to demonstrate you are listening include:

    a. Maintain eye contact to show interest and to observe the speaker.
    b. Lean forward slightly to communicate concern and to better comprehend the message.
    c. Come out from behind a desk or any other physical barrier.
    d. Nod your head to indicate understanding.
    e. Smile when the speaker uses humor.
    f. Allow for pauses—don't feel you have to fill the space with your words while the other person needs time to collect his or her thoughts.

4. **Use open-ended questions to open up communication.** Open-ended questions facilitate the conversation and provide an invitation to respond back and forth. They also let the other person know that his or her thinking is important to you. Open-ended questions begin with words like "Tell me," "What," "How," "Explain," and "Describe."

5. **Use paraphrasing to ensure understanding.** A paraphrase is a brief rephrasing of the speaker's words. Paraphrase by restating the speaker's information in your own words. Paraphrasing shows the speaker that you are listening and that you understand what he or she has said. It also ensures that your interpretation of the message is correct.

    Example:
    "You think the XYZ program is not a good idea because..."

6. **Summarize conversations to ensure understanding and provide closure.** A summary statement is a concise restatement of the key points discussed during a lengthy conversation. The summary brings the conversation to a close. It may also include a recap of specific actions or agreements made.

    Example:
    "As I understand it, you feel that we should bring the marketing people in on this proposal. As we discussed, I will contact them and set up a meeting for next week to discuss their involvement."

Fostering an Open Communication Climate

Speaking clearly and listening for understanding are the first steps to being a more effective communicator. In addition, good managers, supervisors, and leaders take specific actions to create a climate that is conducive to open and honest communication. In this open communication climate, people feel free to give their input and ideas. Information is shared freely and conflicts are openly discussed and worked through. People are more willing to express innovative ideas and to take risks.

The basis of the open communication climate is trust. To begin to build or expand trust in your organization and to foster an open communication climate, try some of the following tips.

1. **Keep your employees informed.** We all want to be "in the know." Take time to keep your employees informed about what is happening within the organization. Let employees in on the "big picture" and the reasons for management decisions. The more people feel informed about their organization, the better they feel about their participation in that organization. When you do not have the answer or are unsure of the reason for a particular decision, be honest with your employees and do whatever you can to get more information to them as soon as possible.

2. **Use a "real" open door policy.** Most managers say they have an open door policy. However, employees often quickly find out that although the door may be open, the mind is closed! If you have an open door policy, it means you welcome people to come to your office with their ideas, comments, complaints, and suggestions.

3. **Encourage others to express contrary viewpoints.** Let people know that you expect them to challenge and disagree with you. When they do, let them state their case. Do not interrupt. Ask questions to ensure that you understand their point of view. Look for areas of agreement and be willing to see others' perspectives.

4. **Don't "shoot the messenger."** Nothing destroys trust and credibility more than this one. A good leader understands that in today's complex organizations people are required to relay messages. All messages should be received calmly and no blame must be placed on the messenger. If you shoot the messenger one too many times, not only will the messenger not come back again, but everyone else will do whatever it takes to keep information from you.

5. **Encourage employees to share information.** If your employees rely solely on you to keep them informed, you will quickly become overwhelmed and the employees will not get all

that they need to do a quality job. Let your staff know that you expect them to share information on a regular basis. Set aside time in staff meetings simply for information sharing. Actively involve others in giving updates and sharing other relevant information. When employees come to you for information that someone else can handle, redirect the employee to go to one of their colleagues for that information.

6. **Use a variety of tools to disseminate information.** Help get the word out by using a variety of tools to communicate. Get your employees' input and suggestions regarding communication tools. You could use such tools as the following:

   a. Departmental bulletin board
   b. Organizational or departmental newsletter
   c. Suggestion box
   d. Special information-sharing meetings
   e. Video or teleconferencing
   f. Electronic mail

7. **Promptly respond to communication from others.** A general rule of thumb is to get back to people within a maximum of twenty-four hours. A better rule of thumb for some of the people would be to get back within four hours. When someone sends you a note, letter, or phone message, get back as soon as you can to let that person know what you are doing about the concern. Even if you cannot respond

with a complete answer or solution right away, you can let them know that you are working on it and that you will get back ASAP. Then, do what you said you would do!

8. **Keep your manager informed.** Take the time to discover what your boss expects from you. How often does he or she expect to hear from you? Does he or she prefer written information (reports or status updates) or a weekly face-to-face meeting? What types of decisions does he or she expect to be consulted on? When can you make decisions on you own? How much detail does he or she like? Remember, just as you would expect from your employees, no boss likes surprises. Find out what your boss needs and keep him or her informed and up to date.

Tips for Success:
Communication

1. Think through what you want to say before you say it. Remember, you cannot *not* communicate.

2. Speak clearly and concisely. Also speak with enthusiasm and expressiveness.

3. Be sincere. Most people have a very fine insincerity detector.

4. Develop an attitude of wanting to listen. Demonstrate this by focusing on the sender's message, not on formulating your response.

5. Use a "real" open door policy with your employees.

6. Show the speaker that you are listening by maintaining eye contact.

7. Use open-ended questions to open up communication.

8. Summarize conversations to ensure understanding and provide closure.

9. Don't shoot the messenger. Encourage or reward people who have contrary viewpoints or who bring you bad news.

10. Keep your boss informed.

6

Delegating to Succeed through Others

*"Never tell a person how to do things. Tell them
what to do and they will surprise
you with their ingenuity."*
General George Patton

Most managers and supervisors have heard about
delegation. We have read about it. We know that it
is important for supervisors to practice. But, like
many of the skills presented in this book, very few
managers or supervisors take the time to study
and practice how to be an effective delegator. Yet to
be successful in their jobs, the concept of
delegation is vitally important to supervisors and
managers.

There are many benefits to effective delegation.

1. **Delegation extends the results from what
   one person can accomplish to what many
   people can accomplish.** By involving others,
   we have the potential to get more things
   accomplished in our area of influence. In
   addition, we are likely to get new ideas and
   approaches to solve problems by tapping the
   input and brain power of others.

2. **Delegation frees up our time to get the most important things accomplished.** Many of the tasks that supervisors and managers do can be completed by their employees. By delegating routine and ongoing tasks, managers will have time for more critical tasks, for leadership activities, and for innovation and problem prevention.

3. **Delegation develops our employees.** When we delegate tasks to employees, we in effect say, "You've got what it takes to do this job." This will enhance levels of trust between the employee and supervisor. Delegation is a critical employee development tool.

4. **Delegation helps to empower our employees by taking the decision-making process to the appropriate level.** Decisions involving problems at different levels of the organization are often better if they are made by the people who are actually doing the work. Making decisions at levels where employees are making the product or dealing with customers fosters motivation and a sense of ownership for the task at hand.

How Are You at Delegating?

How well do you delegate? As a supervisor, answer each question according to your current work structure by circling either a Yes or No response.

Scoring Key: Give yourself one point for each **Yes** answer. A good score is anything above 12.

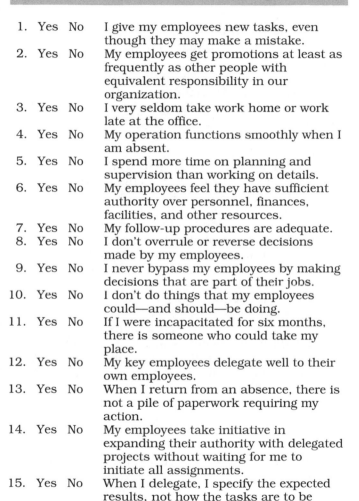

1. Yes No   I give my employees new tasks, even though they may make a mistake.
2. Yes No   My employees get promotions at least as frequently as other people with equivalent responsibility in our organization.
3. Yes No   I very seldom take work home or work late at the office.
4. Yes No   My operation functions smoothly when I am absent.
5. Yes No   I spend more time on planning and supervision than working on details.
6. Yes No   My employees feel they have sufficient authority over personnel, finances, facilities, and other resources.
7. Yes No   My follow-up procedures are adequate.
8. Yes No   I don't overrule or reverse decisions made by my employees.
9. Yes No   I never bypass my employees by making decisions that are part of their jobs.
10. Yes No   I don't do things that my employees could—and should—be doing.
11. Yes No   If I were incapacitated for six months, there is someone who could take my place.
12. Yes No   My key employees delegate well to their own employees.
13. Yes No   When I return from an absence, there is not a pile of paperwork requiring my action.
14. Yes No   My employees take initiative in expanding their authority with delegated projects without waiting for me to initiate all assignments.
15. Yes No   When I delegate, I specify the expected results, not how the tasks are to be done.

Common Mistakes in Delegation and How to Avoid Them

When managers do decide to delegate, there are often mistakes made that can negatively impact the employee's ability to do the job. After reviewing the following common mistakes, determine how you can avoid making these errors.

1. **Display an attitude to the workforce of, "I can do it better myself."** This is prevalent because most supervisors started out doing the job, and often feel that they are still the best person to "do the job"— even though they have been promoted out of the job into supervision. Believe in your employees' abilities. They just might surprise you!

2. **Failure to keep employees informed about plans the supervisor has for the operation.** Some supervisors delegate tasks without providing all the necessary information to do the task successfully. Many supervisors leave out the big picture—the information about future goals, plans, and important organizational decisions. Employees must be fully informed to make the best possible decisions for the organization.

3. **Failure to require, receive, and/or utilize progress reports.** When you do not have a method to check on the employee's progress, two things happen. First, you communicate to

the employee that the task delegated to him or her is not important. Second, you may set yourself and the employee up for failure. Set specific times to check progress from the beginning of delegation through completion. Remember, these checkpoints are designed to help the delegation process, not hinder its success.

4. **Unwillingness to let employees supply their own ideas.** When you do not ask for your employee's ideas and opinions, you are communicating that you do not value the employee. You are also limiting your opportunity to gain new information. Remember, if you always do what you've always done, you'll always get what you've always got! Encourage employees to be creative and give their ideas about ways to complete the task.

5. **Tendency to "dump projects."** Dumping projects usually occurs when the supervisor has not taken the time to plan the delegation properly. So, at a moment's notice, the supervisor assigns the project to the employee. This greatly increases the chances of the project being done incorrectly. To ensure that the delegation is successful, take time to plan the delegation, pick the right person for the job, and discuss the task and its expected outcomes.

6. **Failure to give the employee credit for shouldering responsibility.** Typically, supervisors who do not delegate like to take all the credit in their area of influence. When an employee does take responsibility, no praise or recognition is given by the supervisor. Give credit where credit is due. You will not only gain an enthusiastic employee, but also a loyal one!

7. **Inattention to project completion.** Not recognizing a project's completion will practically guarantee that the next project delegated will be completed late, if at all. This reinforces the supervisor's negative feelings about delegating in the first place. Take a moment to acknowledge task completion. You can also use this opportunity to praise a job well done or to refine or train new skills.

8. **Lack of respect for the employee's ambitions.** Supervisors who do not delegate usually do not have an interest in developing their employees. This leads employees to feel that the supervisor does not care about them. When employees feel that the boss does not care about them, their motivation and respect for their supervisor decreases. So, get to know your employees. Find out their strengths, weaknesses, and their ambitions. If possible, support those ambitions. Help them grow.

Deciding What to Delegate

There are four basic steps in deciding what tasks you presently do that could be delegated:

Step One: Analyze Your Job

The easiest way to analyze your job is to make a list of at least ten tasks that you perform on a daily basis. Create your list in the **"Preparing for Delegation"** form below. The more complete the list is, the better understanding you will have of the tasks you may want to delegate.

Preparing for Delegation

First, list ten of the activities you do on your job.

Activity	Category	Percentage
1.		
2.		
3.		
4.		
5.		
6.		
7.		
8.		
9.		
10.		

Step Two: Categorize Your Activities

Second, categorize each of your activities into one of the following four categories: **RO** for routine or ongoing activities, **FF** for fire-fighting or problem-solving activities, **PR** for proactive or initiative-taking activities, and **ED** for employee development or "helping-people-to-grow" activities. Now, go back and categorize the activities you listed above.

Step Three: Estimate the Percentage of Time in Each Category

Estimate the percentage of time you spend on each activity listed in **"Preparing for Delegation"** and record that amount in the column above marked "Percentage." Then, transfer those amounts into this section below, remembering that the total should add up to 100%.

RO ACTIVITIES	_____
FF ACTIVITIES	_____
PR ACTIVITIES	_____
ED ACTIVITIES	_____
TOTAL:	100%

Research shows that the typical supervisor spends 50% of his or her time on routine activities, another 30 to 40% on fire-fighting activities, and only 10 to 20% on proactive initiative-taking and employee-developing activities. To gain more time for problem prevention and employee development, you have to decide which routine activities you can delegate and to whom.

Step Four: Decide What to Delegate and to Whom

Study the information you have gathered so far, especially concentrating on the RO tasks. Which of these, as well as any of the others, could you delegate? Use **"Planning Your Delegation"** below to help you prepare for delegation.

Planning Your Delegation

List the tasks you could delegate, to whom, by when, and the average number of minutes each day you will save if you delegate the task. In determining who to delegate the task to, consider employee development and learning. Are you selecting the appropriate person for the task?

Task	To Whom	By When	Minutes Saved
1.			
2.			
3.			

The reason we ask you to list the approximate number of minutes you will save each day if you delegate the task is because most people do not realize how a few minutes each day begins to quickly add up. **"Time Value of Delegation"** (below) displays how minutes each day quickly add up into full 8-hour days when considered on a yearly basis.

If you were able to delegate just one task that takes 60 minutes each day, at the end of the year you would have 44 full 8-hour days to be spent another way. That is almost a full month of extra productivity to do more important leadership tasks.

Time Value of Delegation

Minutes Each Day the Task Takes	Number of 8-Hour Days Per Year
15 minutes each day	11 full 8-hour days each year
30 minutes each day	22 full 8-hour days each year
60 minutes each day	44 full 8-hour days each year

Another way to look at this is to ask, "How much is my time or my employees' time worth?" To find out what that means to you, study **"Delegation Savings"** below. Locate your approximate yearly income on the left side of the exhibit and then see what saving an extra hour a day could mean to your success and your organization's profits. When we look at the value of our time, it usually adds up much faster than we think.

Delegation Savings

Yearly Income	Per Hour	Hour a Day All Month	Hour a Day All Year
$20,000	$ 9.62	$202.02	$2,501
$25,000	$12.02	$252.42	$3,125
$30,000	$14.42	$302.82	$3,749
$35,000	$16.83	$353.43	$4,376
$40,000	$19.23	$403.83	$5,000
$45,000	$21.63	$454.23	$5,624
$50,000	$24.04	$504.84	$6,250
$60,000	$28.85	$605.85	$7,501

Note: Income divided by 2080 (52 weeks x 40 hours) for per hour rate. Month as 21 days. Year as 260 days.

Planning to Delegate
Responsibility to the Employee

Now that you have determined what tasks to delegate to whom, take a few moments to plan for the delegation. To do this, you need to answer the following questions:

1. What is the overall goal or purpose of the task?
2. What specific results do I expect?
3. What does the task entail? What specific elements or skills are needed to complete the task successfully?
4. What resources are available to the employee to get the task accomplished?
5. What checkpoints or follow-up agreements need to be made?

Presenting the Delegation

After you have planned for the delegation, you should be clear on your expectations for getting the job done. These expectations must now be made clear to your employee. Keep in mind that your employee is likely to have some good ideas to offer, so plan on soliciting ideas from him or her as well. Below is a process for ensuring delegation success. Be sure to follow each of the seven steps.

Step One: Explain Overall Goal and Purpose

This critical first step lets the employee know the importance and value or relevancy of the task. You will find you get better results if you begin by explaining the big picture, the overall purpose of the task, prior to explaining any of the small details. When employees understand the overall goal, they make better decisions.

Step Two: Outline Expected Results

Once the employee understands the overall goal and importance of the task, he or she needs to know exactly what is expected. Do not get this important step confused with the next step, describing the task. The purpose here is to ensure that you and your employee see the same end result and agree when that result will be in place.

Step Three: Describe Task (optional)

This step is usually for inexperienced employees who have never done the task. You may need to provide some training here. If the task is a large or complex one, break it down into smaller, more manageable pieces for easier explanation. The purpose of this step is to ensure that the employee knows how to do the job. For experienced employees, let them decide. As long as they know the expected results, they can decide how to do the job. And guess what? They may have a better way to do it!

Step Four: Discuss Resources

To do the job effectively, employees need to know what resources are available to them to get the task accomplished. Are they able to purchase equipment or supplies? Are they able to involve other employees? Are they able to enlist the help of other departments? If it takes working overtime, is overtime authorized? Be specific, so the employee is clear on what resources are and are not available.

Step Five: Confirm Understanding; Get Commitment

Here is where you make sure that you made yourself clear. Ask your employee to restate in his or her own words what is expected. You want to do this for two reasons: (1) it involves the employee and (2) you have confirmed knowledge whether the employee understands the task at hand. Encourage the employee to ask any questions to confirm understanding. Last, ask the employee for his or her commitment in completing the task within the agreed-upon time frame. Without commitment, the task may not be done.

Step Six: Ask for Ideas

One of the best ways to empower and motivate your employees is to ask for their ideas. If you tell the employee how you have done the task in the past, make sure you ask him or her for ideas and suggestions on how to complete the task this time. When employees are given the opportunity to provide their own ideas, they take more responsibility for the completion of the task. When you ask for their ideas, be quiet and really listen. Very often a fresh perspective can provide great new ideas, especially if you have "always done it this way."

Step Seven: Establish Follow-Up Plan

The next step is to establish some guidelines for working together. The supervisor always bears ultimate accountability for any delegated task. No supervisor can afford to turn an employee completely loose on a project. To ensure the fulfillment of supervisory responsibilities, a supervisor has to give adequate and proportionate attention to the people delegated the assignments. Schedule follow-ups at certain completion steps throughout the task. Remember, someone at some time in your career gave you room to grow, you made some mistakes, and hopefully, you learned from the mistakes you made. The same process will prove equally valuable to your employees.

Tips for Success:
Delegation

1. To be successful as a supervisor or manager, you have to delegate.

2. Remember that effective delegation will not only expand productivity but will also serve as an employee development tool.

3. List your typical daily activities and determine what percentage are routine, fire-fighting, proactive, or employee development. To be successful, spend more time in the proactive and employee development categories.

4. Calculate the value of your time. Remember, if you delegate a task that only takes you 15 minutes a day, at the end of the year you will have gained 11 full 8-hour days.

5. Plan the delegation. The better your preparation, the better your employees will accomplish the delegated task.

6. When you delegate, present the overall goal and outline the results expected. Do not tell the employee how to do the task, unless he or she is learning for the first time.

7. Discuss what resources are available to get the delegated task completed.

8. Confirm understanding, ask for the employee's ideas, and ask for his or her commitment to get the task accomplished.

9. Establish methods of working together and following up.

10. After you have delegated the task, ensure that the employee maintains ownership of the task.

7

Coaching to Improve Performance

> *"The conventional definition of management is getting work done through people, but real management is developing people through work."*
> Aga Hasan Abedi

Being a supervisor would be so easy if people just did what they were supposed to do! Unfortunately, or fortunately, as the supervisor, you are responsible. It is important to realize that almost all reasons for nonperformance are controlled by the supervisor or manager. Poor performance occurs because of poor supervision. If supervisors and managers took appropriate actions to make sure these reasons for poor performance are prevented or removed, the result would be satisfactory performance.

In this chapter, we will discuss how supervisors can effectively coach and counsel their employees for improved performance. We will also share a proven interactive management process supervisors can utilize to prevent most of the reasons why people do not do what they are supposed to do.

Preparing for the Coaching Discussion

Coaching is, in many ways, a negotiation. And, just like a negotiation session, the better you prepare, the better your chances of obtaining a favorable outcome. Consider the following questions before you begin a coaching discussion. Your answers will provide a framework for conducting a win/win interaction.

1. **What is the problem?** Identify the specific problem. Exactly what is happening that shouldn't be or what should be happening that isn't? Some typical problems may include (a) coming in late, (b) excessive absences, (c) sales down, (d) customer complaints, or (e) incomplete reports. Make sure you define the problem in specific "behavioral" terms. Remember, a bad attitude is not a specific behavioral problem. However, ignoring customers or not providing follow-up within 24 hours is.

2. **What is the cause of the problem?** You may not know for sure what the cause of the problem is until you have the coaching discussion. However, you can begin to identify possible causes. For example, sales may be down because (a) the salesperson is no longer calling on new accounts or (b) maybe existing accounts are not being asked about additional services that may be needed. A clear understanding of the cause of the problem will speed up the problem-solving process and will allow for realistic and practical solutions.

3. **Is the employee capable?** Is the employee physically and mentally able to do the job? Does he or she have the skills, knowledge, and abilities to complete the job or task successfully? If the answer is "no," then education or training may be needed to prepare the employee properly.

4. **Does the employee know right from wrong?** The most common reason employees do not know that they are doing something wrong is because they think they are doing it right. Some supervisors have a bad habit of only providing feedback in severe instances when the employee has demonstrated inappropriate behavior. The other times, when the employee is plodding along on the path of mediocrity, the supervisor says nothing. Many employees think that mediocre performance is good enough because no one has ever told them differently.

5. **Are there rewards for nonperformance or punishments for performance?** A classic example of how an employee could be punished for performance is when a worker in a production facility works faster than the rest of the employees, and as a consequence, is given more work to do. The employees who take their time and work slowly are rewarded by having more work taken away from them. Supervisors experience this phenomenon every day.

Suggestions for Dealing with Performance Problems

If you manage people, no matter how well you do the job, from time to time you will be challenged with performance issues. The following tips will help you deal confidently with the challenges.

1. **Take immediate action.** The longer you wait to confront a negative behavior, the harder it will be to change. It does not take long before the inappropriate behavior becomes a habit, and habits are very hard to break. Once you have determined that a negative pattern of behavior exists, take action.

2. **Give feedback privately.** Prior to beginning the discussion, you should make sure that you have a private location to meet. Take steps to ward off any interruptions. If at all possible, hold the meeting one-on-one. Only in rare instances is a third party necessary. (If the employee is to be terminated or is unwilling to cooperate, you may need a third party, such as a union representative or a human resources representative.)

3. **Remain calm.** If you have ever driven home from work saying, "Now why did I say that?" chances are you may have regretted giving feedback to an employee when you were mad. If you are angry or emotional, postpone the discussion until you are feeling more in control. Remember, communication is

permanent. Do not lose control of the discussion or say something that may later come back to haunt you.

4. **Be consistent.** Do what you say you are going to do. If you tell employees you are going to do something if their inappropriate behavior does not change, do what you say you are going to do. If employees do not feel you are going to take action, they may see no need to change.

5. **Correct behaviors selectively.** Do not use a correcting session to point out all the negative things that you have seen over time. If you coach properly, you should only be dealing with one or two inappropriate behaviors at a time. If you do not have ongoing communication with your employees, you may start to generate a laundry list of behaviors you want to discuss. Our general rule of thumb is, "If it's more than two, they think it's you!" Meaning, if you do bring out your long list of inappropriate behaviors, after about point five or six, the employee begins to think, "Why bother to even come to work? I must not be doing anything right."

6. **Remain positive.** Keep your thoughts positive. Help the employee identify what is causing the problem, and what the employee will do to help resolve the problem. Remember, the goal of this discussion is to make the employee more successful. Only in rare instances is an employee not willing to grow by changing negative behaviors.

Coaching Intervention Models

In working with employees experiencing performance problems, we have found two intervention models to be effective. Both models are discussed below.

Coaching Discussion Model

The purpose of the coaching discussion is to redirect the employee's behavior. You want the employee to stop inappropriate behavior and start demonstrating appropriate behavior. It is a two-way process, a discussion. The intended purpose is for the employee to be engaged in a discussion as well. In fact, the employee should be talking more than the supervisor or the manager. Using the following six steps of the Coaching Discussion Model will make your coaching discussions effective.

Step One: Help the Employee See the Existing Problem

This is the most important step of the entire coaching discussion. If the employee does not agree there is a problem, then the supervisor actually has two problems to deal with: (1) the inappropriate behavior and (2) the employee not thinking the inappropriate behavior is a problem.

Step One is a difficult area for supervisors. Many lack a feeling of competence in this area. Without preparation, this beginning can be difficult;

therefore, many supervisors want to just skip over this step. But, if the employee does not agree there is a problem, he or she will probably lack the motivation to improve behavior.

The types of questions we could ask to gain agreement in this area include:

> *"What is/are the result(s) of this behavior (nonperformance)?"*
> *"What impact does this behavior have on other employees/departments?"*
> *"What would happen if all employees did this behavior?"*
> *"What would happen if I (the supervisor/manager) ignored this behavior indefinitely?"*
> *"Do you know how many times you have done this behavior in the last _____?"*
> *"What impact does this behavior have on our customers?"*
> *"I am puzzled why you don't perceive this as a problem, so can you elaborate?"*

If the employee is still unwilling to admit there is a problem by answering any of the above questions, you may need to move to the second stage of questioning.

> *"What will happen if you continue with this behavior?"*

When the employee responds with, *"You could write me up or suspend me,"* you can then respond with:

> *"You are right. And if you continued with this behavior, after I documented this problem or suspended you, what else could I do?"*

A second question you may try is, *"Do you think I can decide to let you continue this behavior?"*

If the employee states that you can decide to allow the behavior to continue indefinitely, you can respond with:

> *"You are wrong. As a supervisor, I am responsible for seeing that (the area of concern you are discussing) is not a problem in our department/company."*

The employee's comments could activate some of the following responses:

> *"You could suspend, demote, inhibit my promotion, put something in my personnel file, fire me..."*

Your response could be:

> *"You are right, because I need someone in that position who will do (describe the behavior) what needs to be done."*

Some of these questions and responses in this second round sound threatening. If the consequences are realistic—that the employee could be suspended or fired—and if he or she is unwilling to change his or her behavior, it is important that the employee understands the consequences of his or her own behavior.

Step Two: Clarify the Cause of the Problem

Once the employee clearly sees that there is a problem, you can begin to ask "why." The employee may have an idea why the problem is occurring. The employee may know something you don't know. Do not assume that you already know the cause of the problem. Make sure you ask for input and ideas. It is more likely that the person doing the job will have an understanding of why the job is not being done right. This person is also more likely to have good solutions to the problem. As a supervisor, you just need to ask—and then listen.

Step Three: Mutually Discuss Alternative Solutions

Once you have gained agreement that a problem exists and you have clarified the cause of the problem, you are ready to move to solutions. You can say to the employee, "Now that we agree there is a problem, what do you think you can do differently to solve the problem?" Make sure to focus on the word *differently*, because if the employee keeps on doing the same behaviors, he or she will keep getting the same results. It is important that the supervisor lets the employee generate solutions.

Step Four: Mutually Select an Alternative(s)

Do not waste time in Step Three debating which alternative is feasible. If you criticize an alternative an employee shares, the employee will stop sharing. In Step Four, you are now ready to pick an alternative. Once again, the best method to select an alternative is by asking questions. Ask the employee which alternative he or she thinks will work best—and why? Let the employee think it through and let the employee pick the solution.

Step Five: Follow-Up

Make sure to follow up with employees to see how they are doing. Many supervisors make the mistake of not following up to ensure that the agreed-upon action has been taken. The employee will often change the behavior immediately after the performance improvement discussion. But, because there is no recognition for the improved performance, the employee slips back to inappropriate behaviors. Two months later, the supervisor sees the negative behavior again and assumes that there has been no change. If the employee has not modified his or her behavior, the new problem becomes that the employee did not do what he or she agreed to do.

Step Six: Recognize Achievement When It Occurs

If you want the improvement to continue, the key is to recognize it—no matter how small! Recognize the employee's progress. Then, ask the employee what can be done to bring the next round of improvement to an even higher level.

This model is successful in handling the majority of employee-related problems. If you adequately plan for the discussion, you will have positive results. In the rare instances where an employee is still not willing to improve the behavior—even after the discussion—the Corrective Action Feedback Model then becomes appropriate.

Corrective Action Feedback Model

Unlike the Coaching Discussion Model, the Correction Action Feedback Model is not a two-way discussion. While we prefer the discussion model because it is a two-way process involving the employee in both problem identification and solutions to resolve the issue, we find that most supervisors feel more comfortable with the corrective action model. This is a "telling," not an "asking" coaching model. In fact, in this model you actually ask employees to hold their comments and questions until you have finished presenting your information.

Step One: Specifically Describe the Problem Behavior

Example: *"John, in the last month, you have been late to work 15 minutes or more at least five times."*

Step Two: Express Feelings about the Behavior's Impact

Example: *"John, I am disappointed that you continue to come to work late. We have discussed this matter several times. As your supervisor, I feel this is unfair to the other employees who get here on time."*

Step Three: Value the Employee

Example: *"John, you have been in our department for two years. You know the operation well and I value the job that you do."*

Step Four: Specify Desired Future Behavior

Example: *"In the next three months, I am holding you responsible for getting to work on time every day."*

Step Five: Project Positive and Negative Outcomes

Example: *"John, if you are able to be at work on time each day for the next three months, here are the positive things that will happen:*
First, I will quit hassling you about being late.
Second, I will put a letter in your employee file saying that you have improved.
Third, you will be eligible for a favorable performance review.
Fourth, you will once again be eligible for raises and promotions.
Fifth, you will keep your job."

Example: *"John, if you continue to be late, here are the negative courses of action:*
First, we will have this discussion once again. We will document it, and we will place a copy in your employee file.
The second time it happens, I will suspend you for two days without pay.
The third time you are late, you need to understand that I will fire you."

At this point, you must ask the employee if he (John) understands the consequences. If he says "yes," ask him to tell you what he understands. Take this step to make sure that he understands the major points.

There is no arguing that coaching is a tough supervisory skill. However, it is a skill that is critical to your success as a supervisor. No matter how accomplished your team, there will be times when you need to talk to a team member about changing some aspect of his or her performance. So, take time to prepare, envision yourself being successful, and confidently deal with the occasional coaching challenges that come your way. Remember, your ability to lead a great team and progress in your supervisory career will be in direct proportion to your ability to coach your team members.

Tips for Success:
Coaching

1. Focus on behaviors, not on the employee's attitude.

2. Ask great questions; beware of telling an employee about their poor performance.

3. Clearly define performance problems and understand consequences before you go into the performance improvement discussion.

4. Correct immediately. The longer you wait, the harder it gets to change negative behaviors.

5. Correct privately. One-on-one conversation helps to maintain the employee's dignity and respect.

6. Help the employee understand a problem exists by asking questions.

7. Ask the employee for his or her suggestions about how to correct the problem.

8. If possible, allow the employee to select the solution.

9. If you choose to use the Corrective Action Feedback Model, ensure you clarify both the positive and negative outcomes for the employee.

10. Do what you say you are going to do. Ultimately, it will build trust and respect.

8

Conducting Valuable Performance Reviews

> *"Top performers in any field are developed, not born."*
> Joe Griffith

Despite the fact that supervisors typically look for every opportunity to move "Conducting Performance Reviews" to the bottom of their daily "To Do" list, effective performance review systems are a vital part of increasing employee effectiveness. Systems that incorporate a combination of on-the-job coaching, performance appraisals, counseling sessions, interviews, and performance improvement plans developed jointly by supervisor and subordinate can be extremely effective in raising employee performance.

In this chapter, our first goal is to help you become more familiar with the different aspects of a typical performance review system. Our second goal is to help raise your degree of confidence in your ability to conduct employee performance reviews that lead to greater rapport between you and the employees you supervise, and increased employee effectiveness.

Understanding the
Performance Review Cycle

Step One: Clarify Your Expectations

The first step in the review process is to select the significant job elements particular to the employee's position for review and rating. Typical performance appraisals will have five to seven categories, or elements, used to rate employee performance. These job elements should be jointly reviewed and agreed upon by both the supervisor and the employee.

Step Two: Set Performance Standards

Job elements describe what must be done to accomplish the job. Performance standards describe how the job will be done. Together, they provide a guideline for the employee's performance and a basis for reviewing the employee's success on the job. When setting standards for performance, it is important that the employee be involved in the process. This helps ensure that the employee understands the standards and also helps motivate the employee to achieve or exceed the standard. What follows is an example of performance standards for the position of administrative assistant.

Performance Standards

Administrative Assistant

Job Elements	Performance Standards
Answer telephone	Answers calls by the third ring. Takes messages or routes calls to correct voice mail.
Greet visitors	Welcomes visitors and requests they sign in. Gives visitor badge to each visitor. Notifies employee that he/she has a visitor.
Maintain department calendar	Keeps accurate, up-to-date master calendar for all department functions/deadlines. Notifies department employees of significant changes to calendar.
Process incoming mail	Opens correspondence unless marked "confidential." Routes all mail to correct department/employee the same day mail arrives.
File correspondence	All department correspondence filed within three working days of receipt.
Type correspondence and reports	All written correspondence completed by time requested and free of grammatical and spelling errors.

Step Three: Clarify the Rating Scale

Organizations use a variety of rating standards to determine an employee's level of success. The following sample is a simple system used to rate performance:

Job Elements	Performance Standards	Exceeds the Standard	Meets the Standard	Does Not Meet the Standard	Comments
1.					
2.					

Another system commonly used by organizations uses five rating standards:

Job Elements	Performance Standards	Consistently Exceeds Standard	Often Exceeds Standard	Meets Standard	Sometimes Meets Standard	Does Not Meet Standard	Comments
1.							
2.							

When determining a rating system, it is important to describe what each of the gradations used in the system means. For example:

Consistently Exceeds Standard:
> Employee's work consistently exceeds the levels of performance set for this standard.

Often Exceeds Standard:
> Employee's work usually exceeds the levels of performance set for this standard.

Meets Standard:
> Employee's work consistently meets the levels of performance set for this standard.

Sometimes Meets Standard:
> Employee's work is consistently below the levels of performance set for this standard.

Does Not Meet Standard:
> Employee's level of performance is unsatisfactory.

Step Four: The Appraisal Process

During the rating period, the supervisor should be continuously gathering information about the employee's performance. Every attempt should be made to obtain information regarding the employee's performance at regular intervals throughout the rating period, not just the week before the appraisal interview. Evaluating an employee's performance continuously throughout

110

the rating period helps ensure that the information gathered is fair, accurate, and representative of the employee's performance throughout the year.

Documentation

It is important to review the employee's job elements and performance standards periodically and make notes throughout the year regarding the employee's level of performance. This can be as simple as occasionally jotting down a few quick lines noting evidence of either exceptional or unacceptable employee performance. Date the note and drop it into the employee's file.

When it comes time to rate the employee, completing the performance appraisal form will require less time and effort because you have noted levels of performance periodically throughout the year. Further, adequate documentation collected at intervals throughout the year helps ensure that the supervisor remains objective and does not rate the employee based only on performance immediately prior to the end of the review cycle.

Of course, if you have concerns about an employee's performance, do not wait until the end of the performance review cycle to address the issue. Coaching and counseling throughout the cycle is far more effective than waiting until the end of the cycle and then presenting the employee with a list of concerns that you have had throughout the year. Remember, there should be no surprises during the performance review interview. If you have concerns about an employee's performance, the employee should already be aware of these issues.

Self-Appraisal

Some organizations encourage employees to be active participants in the appraisal process by evaluating and rating their own performance prior to the assessment interview with their supervisor. In such organizations, employees are reminded throughout the year to review their standards of performance and document areas where they feel they have exceeded the standard.

Organizations that promote self-appraisal as part of the annual review process cite increased productivity, higher morale, and greater rapport between supervisor and employee as benefits of the program. Employees who participate in the review process are more familiar with their standards of performance for their job and work harder to exceed the standards. Further, employees who complete the self-appraisal are better prepared to actively participate in the review interview.

Step Five: Getting Ready for the Interview

Conducting performance reviews that make a difference and are of value to the employee require thorough prior preparation. Consider the following factors:

112

1. **Think about time and location.** Pick a time of day convenient to both parties and schedule the meeting in an area where the door can be closed and the conversation kept private. Consider also the arrangement of the furniture. If possible, try sitting at a round table, or side-by-side with the employee, which helps equalize the situation and is more conducive to open communication between supervisor and employee.

2. **Complete all required paperwork in advance of the interview.** Make sure that you have reviewed all of your documentation and used it to complete the performance appraisal prior to beginning the interview. If you are going to consider the employee's self-appraisal, leave the actual recording of the rating until you have given the employee time to provide input into the process.

3. **Determine your approach.** It is a good idea to determine, prior to the time the employee arrives, how you will conduct the interview. If the employee has completed a self-appraisal, ask for it now. The most straightforward method for proceeding with the interview is to start at the beginning and go through the job elements one at a time. The supervisor compares his or her rating with that of the employee for each element, and then mutual agreement is reached on the rating for that element. Adequate planning will help you feel prepared and confident as you begin the interview with the employee.

113

4. **Plan your closing.** Remember, what you say last sticks with the employee as he or she leaves and returns to the normal working environment. Plan to summarize the areas where the employee met or exceeded the standard. Offer praise and encouragement, if appropriate. Review areas of concern you may have with the employee's performance. End the interview by encouraging the employee to give some thought to areas where he or she did not meet, or minimally met the standard. Suggest that the employee meet with you again in one week's time to complete a plan of action that will help the employee raise the level of performance in areas where acceptable standards were not met. Plan to end the interview on a positive note, perhaps by conveying to the employee your appreciation for his or her contributions to the company.

Tips for Conducting the Interview

1. **Create a positive climate.** To help the employee relax, it is a good idea to begin the interview with a few minutes of light, easy conversation. Perhaps start with a comment about a recent event at work, a sporting event, or something in the news. Beginning this way helps build rapport with the employee and may help the employee overcome his or her initial nervousness.

2. **Ask questions.** In order to be effective and of value, the employee must be encouraged to talk. Many employees are hesitant about

participating in an annual review, feeling that it is their supervisor's job to determine their ratings and their job to accept the ratings without question. Using open-ended questions such as, "Will you tell me about occasions when you have exceeded this element?" will provide you with further documentation and convey to the employee that the review is a two-way process involving both the boss and the employee.

3. **Listen**. In order to build rapport with the employee, supervisors must not only ask for employee input, but truly *listen*. By that, we mean listen without interrupting and listen with an open mind. While we may have already decided an employee's rating, the employee may be able to present information that will change our perception about his or her performance in a particular area. Listening with an open mind tells the employee, "I value your input," and helps build rapport with the employee.

4. **Focus on performance.** In order to remain objective, avoid such descriptions as "attitude," "not professional," and "unreliable" when describing an employee's performance. These terms are vague, mean something different to everyone, and are hard to measure. Further, employees understandably become defensive when a supervisor tells them they have a "bad attitude" or are "not professional." They immediately begin searching for exceptions to convince you otherwise.

115

Instead, focus specifically on the job elements and the performance standards. Measure the employee's level of performance against the performance standards indicated in the performance review document. People are more receptive to negative feedback when it deals specifically with the standards indicated in the review document. They do not accept negative feedback when it attacks them personally.

Under no circumstances should an employee's performance be compared with the performance of another employee. Comparing employees' performance builds resentment between employees and never achieves the outcome you desire.

5. **Avoid confrontation.** When discussing an employee's level of performance in comparison with the performance standards indicated in the review, avoid confrontation and argument. To get further information, ask questions and listen. Arguing will destroy the rapport you are trying to build with the employee and limit the two-way communication you are trying to establish. Ensuring that communication remains two way helps guarantee that the performance interview will meet the needs of both the supervisor and the employee and result in a "win-win" situation for both people.

6. **Emphasize an employee's strengths.** It is normal to be preoccupied with thoughts about performance areas where you would like to see the employee improve. However, do not

116

overlook the employee's strengths.
Acknowledge what the employee does well and
build on these strengths.

7. **Identify areas for improvement.** Discuss
areas of concern you have with the employee's
performance relative to a particular job
standard. It is important to acknowledge
specifically the performance that does not
meet the standard. For example, you may note
that the employee averages two to three errors
per written page of correspondence. It is
important to have samples of the
correspondence to demonstrate why you are
concerned about the performance. The
acceptable level of performance indicated in
the employee's job standards is "written
correspondence is grammatically correct and
error free."

Other than acknowledging the samples of
errors on the correspondence, do not dwell in
the past. Instead, focus on future employee
performance. For example, you might ask the
employee, "What can you do differently in the
future to avoid these errors that make us look
less than the professionals we are?" Many
employees resent being told how to change
their behavior. If, however, they are permitted
to come up with their own solutions, they are
more committed to making changes in their
behavior that will result in increased levels of
performance.

117

8. **End the performance review interview positively.** It is important to review the employee's strengths before the conclusion of the interview and end on a positive note. Acknowledging acceptable areas of performance helps ensure that the employee will continue to make an effort to meet or exceed the standards. Focusing only on the negative aspects of the employee's performance, or ending the interview on a negative note, will increase the likelihood that the employee will leave thinking, "Why bother? You don't think I'm making a real effort anyway. In the future, you'll get just enough from me so that I can collect my paycheck!"

Step Six: The Performance Improvement Plan

A performance improvement plan describes a course of action taken by both the supervisor and employee that will lead to improved employee performance on the job. During the review interview, job elements in which the employee was not meeting minimum acceptable levels of performance were discussed. The first step in developing an improvement plan is to pick one, or possibly two, job elements to be worked on. Typically, if there is more than one job element requiring improved performance, the most critical one should be chosen first for the plan. (A sample improvement plan is provided at the end of this chapter.)

Tips for Creating the Performance Improvement Plan

1. **Make the plan simple, practical, and easy to understand.** Target one, or possibly two areas, in which the employee needs to improve performance. Provide examples of how the work will improve. For example, "The employee will correctly file all correspondence, using standardized office procedures, within three working days of receipt of the correspondence." When the employee is unsure about where to file the correspondence, he or she will ask a supervisor for specific directions regarding filing the document.

2. **Include specific time lines for targeted behaviors.** To ensure that both you and the employee have a clear understanding of when and how the behavior will be improved, include specifics regarding time. For example, "The employee will answer all incoming calls before the fourth ring. The employee will correctly route all incoming calls within five seconds. If a caller is placed on hold, the employee will verify every thirty seconds that the caller wishes to remain on hold and not leave a message or be connected to voice mail."

3. **Identify training.** Be specific about training that will help the employee improve

119

performance. For example, you may wish to write in the employee's performance improvement plan, "Attend a class on effective telephone techniques during the month of April." "Spend four hours with a customer service supervisor reviewing effective techniques for receiving/routing telephone calls before the end of May." In addition, be specific about whose responsibility it is to arrange the training for the employee.

4. **Demonstrate a positive attitude.** If you are committed to helping the employee identify areas of concern and creating a plan that will help the employee further develop, you will most likely see an improvement in both the employee's behavior and attitude. We are convinced that when supervisors demonstrate a genuine interest in employee development and keep a positive attitude about the employee's ability to improve performance, employees will be motivated to make changes in behavior.

Remember, making changes is tough, and tougher for some employees than others. If an employee is going to improve, there must be a support system in place. The employee may need additional coaching from the supervisor. Additional training may be required. More than anything though, encouragement is needed during a time of change so that the employee will have the confidence to experiment with new ways of doing things.

Sample Personal Improvement Plan

My Personal Improvement Plan
Review Date: _____

1. My areas of strength during the last review
    cycle:

    _____
    _____
    _____

2. The job elements where I need to improve my
    performance:

    _____
    _____

3. My goals for improving my performance:

    _____
    _____
    _____

4. Action steps needed for me to accomplish my
    goals:

Action	**Who Is Responsible?**	**When**
_____	_____	_____
_____	_____	_____
_____	_____	_____

_____ _____
Employee Signature   Supervisor Signature

_____ _____
Date   Date

In conclusion, the most important aspect of any performance review process is obviously not the format or technique utilized, but the underlying attitude by which both the employee and supervisor view the entire process. When supervisors view performance evaluation as part of an ongoing process which can positively lead to improved employee performance, there are far-reaching benefits not only for the individual, but also the organization as a whole. Supervisors with this perspective no longer view conducting performance reviews as "the job that nobody wants!"

Tips for Success:
Performance Reviews

1. Gather examples of performance, both positive and negative, throughout the year, not just the two weeks before the performance appraisal is due.

2. Be positive. Remember to include documentation showing where the employee is doing a great job, not just in areas where there is room for improvement.

3. Make sure you are familiar with all the performance standards and rating criteria for the job before conducting the review process with the employee.

4. Plan your schedule so that you will not be interrupted when giving feedback to the employee. Doing so demonstrates respect for the employee and the process.

5. Pick a quiet, private location and give consideration to the seating arrangements. When possible, come out from behind your desk.

6. Ask for employee input. Listen. Listening conveys you care and value the employee's insights.

7. Focus on behavior. Remember, people cannot change their personalities, but can change their behavior.

8. Be specific about what improved performance looks like. Use examples.

9. Remember to look for positive changes in employee behavior and recognize the employee's success.

10. Put a date on your calendar to remind you to check back with the employee who is working on an improvement plan.

9

Building a High-Performing Team

"A house divided against itself cannot stand. There are only two options regarding the commitment to teamwork. You're either In or you're Out. There is no such thing as life in-between."
Pat Riley, Coach of the Miami Heat

One of the challenges that every supervisor and manager has is the task of bringing people together to function as a team. In today's competitive environment, supervisors need to decide what will enable their work group to provide the highest level of quality, customer service, or task accomplishment. Although there are rare exceptions, in most situations, the ability to respond to quality and customer service is much stronger when people operate as a team.

Teamwork Defined

A team is a small group of people (ideally consisting of between five to seven members) with complementary skills who are committed to working with each other toward a common purpose. It is important to recognize that just because you are a supervisor with a specific group of people assigned to complete a specific organizational task, that does not necessarily mean you are leading a team. A team is not just any group working together. Groups do not become teams just because someone labels them a team. If any significant piece of the preceding definition is lacking, then what you have is a group of people who work together.

What Makes a Great Team?

In both our consulting practice and research, we have uncovered five characteristics that are common among all great teams.

1. **Great teams have a common, shared goal.** Team members are equally committed to a common purpose, goals, and working approach for which they hold themselves mutually accountable. As a supervisor or manager, you have the opportunity to set the goals for your team. This technique is used by the majority of supervisors. The supervisor tells the team what needs to be accomplished and how to accomplish the task, whether on this shift or in a specific work period. People need to know what needs to be accomplished.

2. **The team has a positive vision of what the team is trying to accomplish.** The term "vision" can be clarified as a clear mental picture of a desired future outcome. Someone on the team, either the supervisor, leader, or

126

other team member is able to convey a positive vision of the team's results. As a supervisor, whether you have a positive or negative vision of the future, you will be influential. For example, if you as the team leader *do not* have a positive vision of your team's ability to accomplish the goal, and no one on your team does either, there is a strong chance you will all be right!

3. **Great teams are driven by performance challenges.** It is the challenge that energizes a team to greatness, regardless of its location in the organization. A common set of demanding performance goals, or a significant accomplishment that needs to be completed, or a large problem that is having a negative impact on both people and the organization will usually result in both high performance and a strong team. As a supervisor or manager, you need to ensure that your team is working on a challenging goal that is meaningful to each member of the team.

4. **Great teams value and respect the contributions of each member.** Team members need to recognize that each individual brings a unique gift or contribution to the team. Also, it is important that each team member recognizes that it would be harder to accomplish the task without each individual's unique contribution.

5.   **Great teams win.** It does not matter whether
     you are on a sports team or in a business
     environment, great teams accomplish their
     goals or tasks. It is your challenge as a
     supervisor or manager to build a winning
     team. Anyone could win by being given ten
     ideal or perfect employees to do the job. The
     problem is that in real life this never happens.
     And an even bigger problem might be that if it
     did happen, there would be *no* need for the
     supervisor!

Stages of Team Development

Stage One: Formation

In this first stage, it is actually safe to say that you
have a group of people who work together, rather
than a true team. People in this stage will gather
together to share information, or to decide what
actions will help individuals better fulfill their
specific job functions, but there is not a committed
focus toward a common goal. Some of the key
characteristics of groups in this stage include:

> Lack of honest communication
> Members are watchful and guarded
> Minimal group work accomplishment
> Learning new jobs and roles
> Hesitant participation
> Uncommitted people
> Unspoken concerns
> Unclear roles and responsibilities

If you were the team leader observing these characteristics on your team, the question becomes, "What can I do to help move the team forward?" The following five suggestions will help move a team through the team development process.

1. **Meet often.** When new teams come together, team members feel a lack of "belonging" to the team. Because of this lack of belonging and the unknown relationships, along with unclear roles and responsibilities, it is sometimes easier for individuals not to meet at all. Everyone will go on doing their own jobs without feeling a need to come together as a team. By meeting more often in the beginning of team development, the members get to know and trust each other earlier in the proccss.

2. **Conduct introductions.** If people do not know each other well, it will be helpful to have people introduce themselves. As the leader, it is your responsibility to give people an opportunity to get to know each other.

3. **Give a proper orientation to the team.** Any time a new member joins a team, this addition has the potential to send the team back to the forming stage. It is helpful to give new members the proper history and background of your team.

4. **Clarify team goals.** We know that one of the key characteristics of a great team is a challenging goal. It is important that all team members have been involved in the goal setting and clarification process.

5. **Ask for commitment.** When teams are new, we do not know who is really committed to the team's goals and who is not. You will find it helpful to ask people directly for the commitment to helping the team be successful. You may also find it helpful to ask team members what they would like to personally achieve by being a member of the team.

Stage Two: Conflict

As members get accustomed to working with each other, conflict or feelings of hopelessness or helplessness may arise. We have listed some of the outward characteristics of this stage of team development:

Blaming
Competition
Lack of trust
Infighting
Whining
Feeling stuck
Polarization (i.e., day shift vs. night shift)
Minimal work accomplishment

These characteristics are not bad, but rather a natural course of direction in the team-building process. As the supervisor or manager, it is part of your job to know what you can do to help move the team forward. The following five suggestions provide specific guidance.

1. **Address team members in conflict.** The worst thing you can do when conflict arises on your team is to ignore it. You may ask two team members to sit down and resolve their conflict, or you may sit down and play the role of a mediator in resolving the conflict. Either way, you are addressing the conflict, rather than ignoring it.

2. **Maintain conversations in the aim frame.** We advise supervisors in our seminars to be "aim frame thinkers" vs. "blame frame thinkers." Aim frame thinkers ask two questions: "Where do we want to be?" and "How do we get there?" These two questions keep all conversations healthy and productive. Blame frame thinkers also address two questions: "What's wrong?" and "Who can we blame?" With these last two questions we only have two guarantees—nothing will be accomplished and it will divide the group.

3. **Meet often.** Groups in conflict will actually stop meeting because they would rather avoid each other than discuss the conflict. Force the group to meet and discuss the sensitive issues. If you stick to the aim frame, it will go well.

4. **Ask participants to sit in different seats.**
   Groups in conflict have set seat assignments
   that many times they will refuse to change
   because that may mean they have to sit next
   to someone they do not like. Prior to each
   meeting, tell people they have to sit in a
   different seat next to someone new. In fact,
   you might even lead by example. It works!

5. **Focus on results.** This is the stage when
   many managers spin their wheels
   concentrating on making the relationships
   "right." You may find it more productive to
   focus your energy on the results the team
   produces. When the team members are totally
   focused on results and are held accountable
   for the results, many of the relationship
   problems will be resolved by the individuals
   involved.

Stage Three: Functional Work Group

This stage occurs when teams get their jobs done.
There is not a lot of conflict, but then again, there
is not a lot of excitement either. Teams come
together each day, do their assigned duties, and
then leave. Some of the key characteristics of this
stage include:

> Getting organized
> Establishing procedures
> Displaying team cohesiveness
> Using interactive dialogue
> Confiding in each other
> Confronting issues as a team

132

You may ask the question, "If the team is not broken, why try to fix it?" The reason is because a team in this stage is capable of much more. With a few adjustments, you can help to improve the level of commitment, the level of productivity, and the amount of fun and satisfaction individuals gain by being a part of the team. Some actions to help the team move forward include:

1. **Set new goals.** If the team is comfortable where they are, see if the team can come up with any new challenges. It is during the times when we are challenged that we succeed and do our very best.

2. **Provide training.** In the functional work group stage, people may begin to feel like they have stopped growing. Find out what people would like to learn and help them promote their personal and professional growth.

3. **Encourage innovation.** This is the stage when you will hear the line, "But we have always done it that way, why change?" Change creates growth in individuals and teams, and growth helps to increase satisfaction.

4. **Recognize what is right.** In this stage, supervisors tend to become involved when something is not right. This means that people only hear from you when something is wrong. Make a commitment to also recognize those things that are going well.

Stage Four: A High-Performing Team

This is the stage where the definition of teamwork, listed at the beginning of this chapter, fully develops. You will begin to see some of the key characteristics of a high-performing team:

> Members care about each other
> High energy
> Aim frame discussions
> Closeness
> Common vision and purpose
> Fun as a team
> Creative problem solving
> High trust among team members
> Continuous improvement

This time, the discussion is not centered around what can you do to move the team forward, but rather, what can you do to help keep the team performing at high levels. Some ideas include:

1. **Celebrate successes.** In watching great teams perform, we have observed that they will find a reason to celebrate every success. Part of their motivation is knowing they will recognize the superior accomplishments of the team.

2. **Do a team audit.** When things are going great, most people will feel comfortable addressing the question, "What could we have done even better?"

3.   **Change your role to facilitator.** High-
     performing teams will operate whether the
     leader is present or not. Knowing that, become
     a facilitator, rather than the "supervisor."
     High-performing teams know what needs to be
     done.

4.   **Set new goals and vision.** If the group is not
     continually setting new challenging goals, the
     team will lose its drive and motivation. People
     want to be a part of a team that is
     accomplishing something great.

5.   **Have fun.** There is no greater reward than
     being a part of a fun team!

   Assessing Your Skills as a Team Leader

The following checklist provides you with a quick
assessment of your current ability as a team
leader. The 15 items outline some key abilities
required for leading a team.

Checklist for Team Leadership Skills

Read each statement and then place a check on the line after the appropriate number to indicate your current ability. Ratings run from 1 (low) to 10 (high). Respond as you think a consensus of your team members would score your abilities.

Low   **High**

1. I set measurable goals.
   1__ 2__ 3__ 4__ 5__ 6__ 7__ 8__ 9__ 10__

2. I really listen to others.
   1__ 2__ 3__ 4__ 5__ 6__ 7__ 8__ 9__ 10__

3. I give clear directions.
   1__ 2__ 3__ 4__ 5__ 6__ 7__ 8__ 9__ 10__

4. I develop trust with and among others.
   1__ 2__ 3__ 4__ 5__ 6__ 7__ 8__ 9__ 10__

5. I inspire positive team performance.
   1__ 2__ 3__ 4__ 5__ 6__ 7__ 8__ 9__ 10__

6. I confront conflict in a positive manner.
   1__ 2__ 3__ 4__ 5__ 6__ 7__ 8__ 9__ 10__

7. I remain objective when someone disagrees with me.
   1__ 2__ 3__ 4__ 5__ 6__ 7__ 8__ 9__ 10__

8. I keep meetings on topic.
   1__ 2__ 3__ 4__ 5__ 6__ 7__ 8__ 9__ 10__

9. I effectively manage time in a meeting.
   1__ 2__ 3__ 4__ 5__ 6__ 7__ 8__ 9__ 10__

10. I provide a clear vision to team members.
    1__ 2__ 3__ 4__ 5__ 6__ 7__ 8__ 9__ 10__

11. I effectively delegate work to others.
    1__ 2__ 3__ 4__ 5__ 6__ 7__ 8__ 9__ 10__

12. I establish positive relationships with key employees and customers.
    1__ 2__ 3__ 4__ 5__ 6__ 7__ 8__ 9__ 10__

13. I am able to influence upper management.
    1__ 2__ 3__ 4__ 5__ 6__ 7__ 8__ 9__ 10

14. I am patient with people who are slow or who challenge me.
    1__ 2__ 3__ 4__ 5__ 6__ 7__ 8__ 9__ 10__

15. I recognize the stages of team development and am able to move the team through the stages.
    1__ 2__ 3__ 4__ 5__ 6__ 7__ 8__ 9__ 10__

Effective team leaders must realize that they don't know all the answers, and that they cannot succeed without other members of the team. Work on improving any "Low" ratings and maintain or even reinforce the skills of "High" ratings.

Leading Your Team Out of a Crisis

From time to time, every supervisor or manager will find they are in charge of a team in crisis. Crises come in many shapes and sizes. A few we have seen supervisors struggle with include: team members who do not get along, company financial problems, morale or motivation at an all time low, quality problems, customer service problems, departments at war with each other, and top management not supportive of a team or department.

The deeper the crisis, the more challenging it is for supervisors and managers to figure out how to solve the problems and put the team back on track. Many times, supervisors and managers do not know what action they should take. Because of this lack of definite action, the supervisor or manager "hopes" that the situation will get better on its own. We can say that very seldom does the team come out of crisis on its own when the supervisor or manager is using the action of "hope." The following ten action steps will help you lead your team out of a crisis:

1. **Face reality.** When a crisis hits and supervisors/managers are not sure what to do, the first inclination is to deny that the problem is as big as it really is. The animal that comes to mind is the ostrich. If we bury our head in the sand, the problem will not seem as large as it really is. But just like the ostrich, when we stick our head in the sand, we leave other parts of our body exposed. Face reality—the problem most likely will not go away unless you do something to solve the crisis.

2. **Take action.** If you wait until your boss helps to solve the problem or until team members decide to help solve the problem, you may wait forever. Be empowered. You have the ability to take responsibility to make decisions and actions that will lead the team from crisis. If you are not empowered to do this, then there is a good chance your team is going to remain in crisis.

3. **Prioritize.** When teams fall into a crisis, there are usually many problems that may be impacting the team. You cannot fix all the problems at once so it is in your best interest to get the team involved and prioritize the actions that need to be taken. If the team is unwilling to prioritize actions, then you will have to decide which problems to solve and in what order.

4. **Focus on results.** When teams are in crisis, there is a tendency to focus on trying to fix the relationships that have broken down. While the thought or attempt is good, we have found it much more productive for floundering teams to focus on results. When everyone is focused on the purpose of the team and the results it must produce, many of the relationship problems will resolve on their own. If the team is not productive, there will always be relationship struggles.

5. **Recruit the cream of the crop.** When teams go into crisis, it is usually the very best team members who leave. Unfortunately, the most challenging team members never seem to leave. In a crisis, analyze your people assets and spend time asking the top performers to band with you and help solve the problems. Most people will stay in a bad situation if they know they can help improve the crisis, feel valued, and have a positive vision that tomorrow will be better than today.

6. **Praise and recognize your people often.** The reason we emphasize this as a specific point is because when a team goes into crisis mode, and you are the leader of this team, you tend to focus your energy on what is going wrong instead of recognizing all the things that are going right. When people do not feel valued, and the team or organization is in a crisis, you start to hear team members say, "I don't get paid enough to put up with this garbage." One way we can minimize this feeling in our team members is to value their contributions and recognize them for doing things right.

7. **Tighten discipline.** When teams go into crisis, there are usually many things happening that are not conducive to good teamwork. When a crisis occurs, it is in your best interest as a supervisor or manager to tighten, not loosen discipline. This means you need to hold people accountable for coming to work on time, providing high quality service, or producing quality parts. Without tightening the boundaries or setting detail standards, you send out messages to all team members that negative behaviors are acceptable.

8. **Identify who is responsible and what role that individual will play.** In a moment of crisis, it is critical that you clarify who is responsible and what role that individual will play in leading the team from crisis. This point helps to keep focus on the results. When a team is in crisis, you will usually find that

team members are clear on what is wrong and who is to blame, but they are not clear on what needs to be done and who is responsible. As the supervisor, you can assign roles and responsibilities.

9. **Overcommunicate.** When a supervisor or manager is "in" over his or her head with team problems, there is a tendency to focus energy on operational, rather than leadership, tasks. You begin to utter these words, "All I do around here is put out fires." As a supervisor, your primary role is to support others. Increase your communication to team members, both information provided by you and information given to you from the team. Most of the time, your team has the ability to solve the problems if you utilize them as a resource. Increase your communication in a crisis and it will lessen the negative impact of the crisis.

10. **Maintain a positive mental attitude.** If you throw in the towel because you feel the situation is hopeless, then most likely your team members will view the situation as hopeless also. Not having a positive mental attitude can have a negative impact on a supervisor's or manager's career. If you have no hope of the situation getting better, but someone else does, either on the team or in the organization, your team members will begin to follow someone else. A supervisor or manager with no followers is not a leader.

141

We are the first to agree...teams are not for everyone or every situation. Nonetheless, teams usually outperform other groups or individuals. And, teams perfect individual members' strengths and overcome their weaknesses.

Tips for Success:
Team Performance

1. Great teams have a clear mission, vision, and great goals. Make sure your team has a common, challenging goal that makes team members stretch to reach it.

2. Create an environment where the contributions of all team members are recognized and valued, not just the "stars."

3. Don't oil the squeaky wheel. Value creativity. Recognize and reward those that challenge "the way we always do things around here."

4. Confront conflict. If you stick your head in the sand and deny it exists, remember what part of you is exposed!

5. At every opportunity, try switching from being a directive leader to a team facilitator.

6. Promote cross-training to multiply the number of "experts" on your team.

7. Set goals with specific deadlines. Goals without deadlines are only a "hope."

8. People need to feel they belong. Praise and recognize your people frequently.

9. Success is not permanent. Focus on recruiting the cream of the crop as you anticipate the need for new team members.

10. Celebrate success!

10

Selecting and Hiring Winners

> *"The world is full of willing people; some willing to work, the rest willing to let them."*
> Robert Frost

One manager recently confided to us, "I don't know much about wrongful terminations, but I sure have made some wrongful hires in my time!" In the previous chapters, we have discussed the skills needed to manage employees effectively once they are on the job. In this chapter, we will review the skills needed to hire the right people. When the right person is in the right job, it makes all the other skills we have discussed in this book much easier to practice.

As preparation for this topic, try the assessment tool below.

Interviewing Skills Self-Assessment

There is no grading scale for this assessment. If you circle a high number of "Yes" responses, you need to practice and learn effective interviewing skills.

Yes   No   1.   Have you ever hired a person who did not have the skills you thought they had?

Yes   No   2.   After the interview, have you ever thought of something you wish you had told the candidate?

Yes   No   3.   When the interview is complete, are you still confused about the candidate's qualifications?

Yes   No   4.   Of the five people you have most recently hired, have any left for employment elsewhere?

Yes   No   5.   Have you ever asked a question of a candidate and then later found out that the question was not legal to ask?

Yes   No   6.   Do you ever find that you do not have time to prepare adequately for the interview?

Yes   No   7.   Do you tend to do more talking than the candidate?

Yes   No   8.   Have you ever found you did not hear the candidate's response because you were thinking of what question to ask next?

Yes   No   9. After the interview, have you ever
                 thought of something you wish you
                 had asked the candidate?

Yes   No   10. Have you ever protected your
                 nervousness by sitting behind your
                 desk or some other comfort zone of
                 authority to conduct the interview?

Conducting the Interview

When conducting the interview, an organized
approach must be followed if you want to get all
the information you need in the allotted time. The
following organizational format will ensure that you
get to the most critical questions.

1. **Welcome/greeting.** The purpose is to
    welcome the applicant and put him or her at
    ease. Welcome the applicant with a smile and
    a handshake. Introduce yourself. Offer coffee,
    water, or other refreshment and guide the
    applicant to the interview location. Once you
    are both seated and ready to begin the
    interview, start the conversation with "small
    talk" to get the applicant to talk, "break the
    ice," and "open up." This might include, "How
    was the traffic coming in this morning?" or any
    other noncontroversial area of general interest.

2. **Interview structure preview.** The purpose is
    to let the applicant know what to expect and
    reduce anxiety about the interview process.

147

The preview could go something like this: "Well, because we don't have much time today, I'd like to get started on the interview. Let me tell you what I have planned. I'd like to start with your work experience and then talk about your education. After that, I'll ask you to give me a self-assessment of your strengths and development needs. Then, I'll take some time to answer your questions and to give you more information about the position and our company."

3. **Work experience.** The purpose is to get specific information, examples, and illustrations of the applicant's work experience, job skills, and knowledge.

   Ask questions to get details about what type of work was done, how it was done, and what results were achieved. Ask follow-up and probing questions to get more details. For example, if the applicant says that one of his or her previous duties included training, a series of follow-up questions might include:

   "How did you go about determining the content for the training?"
   "Give me an example of one of the key training points and how you presented it."
   "What kind of results did you achieve with the training?"
   "How did you measure your success?"
   "What might you do differently if you had the chance to do it over again?"

4. **Education.** The purpose is to understand the applicant's specific education and training and to see how their education relates to the necessary job requirements. You are asking the applicant to "tell the story" of his or her educational background.

5. **Self-assessment.** The purpose is to get the applicant's perspective of his or her own strengths and development needs. Ask the applicant to give you his or her perspective of what he or she considers to be personal strengths and the areas needing improvement. In areas noted for improvement, ask the applicant what he or she is doing to grow in this area.

6. **Present information and answer questions.** The primary purpose of this segment is to "sell" the employee on the job. At this point, you will have a good idea if this seems to be the right person for the job. If this is a top candidate, discuss the advantages of the job and how it benefits the applicant. If you will not be seriously considering the applicant, you will not need to spend much time in this area. However, you do need to complete this section to ensure a fair interview and to promote good public relations.

7. **Close the interview.** Determine if the applicant is interested in the position by asking directly, "What is your level of interest in the position?" Explain the next steps. This

149

could include who else you would like the applicant to interview with; when they will be notified about the next interview; or when the hiring decision will be made. End the interview on a positive note by thanking the applicant for taking the time to speak with you. Do not make an offer or a rejection statement at this time. You will need some time to analyze your interview notes and to think through the process.

The Art of Questioning

The primary goal of the interview is to get the best information possible so the interviewer can make a good selection. The best tool for getting good information is to ask good questions. There are two different types of questions: close-ended questions and open-ended questions.

1. **Close-ended questions.** Close-ended questions are questions that can be answered with a *yes* or *no*. For example, if you asked an applicant if he or she likes his or her present job, the answer could simply be *yes* or *no*. The disadvantage of using close-ended questions in an interview is they do not produce the maximum amount of possible information. Close-ended question begin with words like "Is," "Can," "Do," "Did," "Will," and "Are."

2. **Open-ended questions.** Open-ended questions are questions that need expansion to be answered. They usually start with words

like "What," "Where," "When," "Why," "How," "Tell me," "Explain," and "Describe." The advantage of using open-ended questions is that you will receive more information rather than less. For example, if I ask, "Tell me what you really like about your present job?" I am going to receive much more information than if I asked, "Do you like your current job duties?"

The following examples illustrate how you can change close-ended questions (CL) to open-ended questions (OP).

CL   Do you have good communication skills?
OP   What do you feel your key strengths are in the area of communication?

CL   Were you attracted to work here because of our benefits?
OP   What attracted you to seek employment with our company?

CL   Did you make any major mistakes in your last job?
OP   Can you describe a major learning point from your previous jobs?

CL   Have you ever had a personality clash with a boss?
OP   Tell me what you have liked and disliked about previous bosses.

CL   We have a very fast-paced environment here. Are you motivated?
OP   What type of business environment do you enjoy best?

There are many other useful open-ended questions for interviewing purposes.

> *How would you describe your past job in detail?*
> *Tell me how you spend a typical day on the job.*
> *Why do you want to leave your present job?*
> *What are your greatest strengths?*
> *What are your biggest weaknesses?*
> *What are you doing to overcome them?*
> *On your past jobs, what significant contributions did you make?*
> *What specific tasks do you enjoy most? Why?*
> *What specific tasks do you like least? Why?*
> *Tell me about the most challenging project you have ever had to tackle.*

Open-ended questions are powerful questions because they do not lead the applicant in a specific direction. For example, if you asked the question, "Do you enjoy working on computers?" what candidate would disqualify himself or herself by saying *no*? But, if you asked an open-ended question like, "Tell me what you disliked in your last job?" and the applicant responds that he or she disliked working on the computer all day, you have a pretty sound indication this may not be the best applicant for a position that requires extensive computer work.

Avoid Common Errors

In preparing for the interview, it is helpful to be aware of some of the most common errors that interviewers frequently make.

1. **Talking too much.** Studies indicate that most interviewers talk 50% or more of the time during an interview. An interview that is dominated by the interviewer fails to accomplish the most crucial purpose of the interview—to get information from the applicant. An effective interviewer will conduct the interview so that he or she spends only about 20% of the time talking and the applicant spends 80% of the time talking.

2. **Telegraphing the desired response.** Interviewers often lead or help the candidate get the "right answer" by telegraphing the answer that they want to hear. For example, the interviewer says, "How do you feel about working on teams? We have a very strong work ethic around here that values teamwork." Now, what would you say to this? "No, I think teams are a lousy idea!" Make sure that your questions are straightforward and do not telegraph the desired response.

3. **Failing to know job requirements.** You cannot conduct an effective interview without first knowing the specific job requirements. This is where effective preparation pays off. Take the time to conduct a thorough job

analysis that will clarify specific job duties, responsibilities, skills, knowledge, and abilities.

4. **Jumping to conclusions.** Interviewers often make the mistake of making quick judgments and jumping to conclusions before they have enough information to make a sound decision. If the applicant says one thing that does not fit with what you are looking for, it does not mean that they are not the right person for the job. On the other hand, if an applicant says something that you are very impressed with, this should not be the single contributor to your decision to offer the job.

5. **Reacting to the "halo" effect.** This common mistake is made when the interviewer happens to really "like" the applicant. Sometimes you will just "hit it off" with someone. This is when an interviewer may make the hasty judgment that this applicant would be "perfect" for the job. Beware, you may be under the *halo effect.* You have put a "halo" over the head of the applicant. He or she can do no wrong—even though he or she may be *wrong* for the job.

6. **Being disorganized.** Interviewers who do not take a systematic approach to the interview will be disorganized and may lose valuable time to get the information they need. Effective interviewers take an organized approach and plan out the interview sequence. This pre-planned structure ensures that the interviewer

will be able to cover what is needed to make the best possible selection determination.

Making the Hiring Decision

Now that you have taken the time to plan and conduct a thorough interviewing process, you are ready to make the selection decision. Because you have carefully analyzed the job, you will be able to screen out unqualified applicants quickly and select from the most qualified candidates.

Even with the extensive data you have, you may find it difficult to decide among the top two or three candidates. You may want to go through a rating and ranking process, assigning numerical measurements so you can "add up" the qualifications of each candidate and select the candidate with the highest rating.

1. Ask some additional questions to make the final decision.

    a. Accomplishments. What was really accomplished on previous jobs?
    b. Responsibilities. Is this level of responsibility right, too high, or too low?
    c. Skills and knowledge. Does the candidate have what it takes to do the job?
    d. Strengths. Are the key strengths present? Will these strengths add to the position?
    e. Weaknesses. Does each specific limitation impact the job? Is it offset by a necessary strength? Can this weakness be remedied

through a brief orientation, learning on
the job, or other training?

f.   Stability. Is this an important factor or
not?

g.   Compatibility. Will this candidate be
compatible with others in your
department? Others in the organization?

h.   Past behavior. Is there repeated evidence
or a pattern of successful performance?

Interviewing and hiring the right candidate is a
challenging and time-consuming activity. At times
you may be tempted to make a quick selection just
to get someone "on board" quickly, even though
you may have some apprehensions. Based on some
painful previous experiences when we made some
hasty decisions, we know that the more time you
spend in the selection process, the higher your
level of success. Further, the time spent in
searching for the right person is insignificant
compared to the time spent trying to rid yourself of
a "wrongful hire!" Commit to taking all stages of
the interview and selection process seriously so
that you consistently hire "winners" for your team.

Tips for Success:
Selection Process

1.   Take time to understand your organization's
hiring process.

2.   Remember, the three primary purposes of the
hiring interview are (1) get information, (2) give
information, and (3) promote good public
relations.

3. Take time to plan the interview.

4. Let the job applicant talk. Plan on spending 80% of the time listening and 20% talking.

5. Do not give away the answers you expect by telegraphing the desired response.

6. Conduct a job analysis—know the job requirements.

7. Get the whole picture. Avoid jumping to conclusions.

8. Use open-ended questions to get complete and thorough answers.

9. Know the law and ensure that you conduct fair and legal interviews.

10. Start your new employee off on a positive note by providing a warm welcome and thorough orientation.

11

Facilitating Productive Meetings

"Meetings do not need to be punishment. After all, gatherings to discuss a subject of common interest are what parties are all about."
Philip B. Crosby

Ask any group of managers and supervisors to list their top three most time-consuming activities and "unproductive meetings" always surfaces in their lists. These same managers and supervisors regretfully admit that about half their time in meetings is wasted. Unfortunately, we never know ahead of time which half of the meeting is going to be the productive half. If it were known, we could plan accordingly and better manage our time!

To Meet or Not to Meet?

The first step in planning a successful meeting is to make an important decision. The decision is whether or not to even hold a meeting. Many meetings should **not** occur at all. Meetings that are called because a manager is unable or unwilling to make a decision are examples of meetings that should not take place. Another inappropriate reason is to call a meeting simply for the sake of meeting. In today's world of information overload, to meet without a specific purpose is inexcusable.

Planning a Productive Meeting

Step One: Creating the Agenda

After determining whether a meeting needs to be held, and if it does, what type, the next step is to begin the planning. Every meeting should have an agenda. An agenda sends participants the message that their time is valued enough to do prior planning. It also lets participants know ahead of time what they will be doing during the meeting. Participants then have an opportunity to prepare themselves for the meeting. They can make sure that they have all the data needed to make an informed contribution to the meeting. (To help you plan and conduct a productive meeting, a checklist is provided at the end of this chapter.)

An agenda should include the following:

1. **Start time.** Establish a start time and then begin right on time. Starting on time rewards those who are prompt and ready to start at the announced time. When you have a reputation for starting on time, people attending your meetings will show up on time!

2. **Topics.** The topics to be covered at the meeting should be listed next, in the sequence in which they will be discussed during the meeting. Be brief here, including only enough information for participants to be able to identify the subject.

3. **Break time.** If a meeting is scheduled to run more than 90 minutes, schedule a short break. When participants start their break, be very specific about the time you will resume. Start again promptly at the announced time. People will get the message that you value their time and intend to keep the meeting moving productively.

4. **Summary.** End every meeting with a short summary of the topics covered and the outcome. Although this activity doesn't take long, it helps participants focus on the content of the meeting and reminds them that the meeting accomplished something.

5. **Follow-up.** After the summary, review participants' future responsibilities. Whatever participants have agreed to contribute needs to be reviewed before the meeting adjourns, whether it be assuming responsibility for a task or gathering more information for a future meeting.

6. **Adjournment time.** Stick to your agenda. Work hard to keep the meeting progressing towards the established goals. End on time. As with starting on time, ending meetings on time will quickly build your reputation for being an organized leader with respect for others' time.

Step Two: Selecting the Participants

Generally, when deciding who should participate, the smallest number of appropriate people is the best guideline to follow. If it is to be an informational meeting, the participants will include all those who need the information. On the other hand, if the meeting will have a problem-solving format, then you should consider the following criteria when you select participants. Participants attending problem-solving meetings should have:

1. **Expertise in the problem.** Select participants who have knowledge or technical expertise in the area that will be considered during the meeting.

2. **Commitment.** Participants should have a mutual interest in solving the problem, therefore they will be committed to the problem-solving process.

3. **Diversity.** When selecting participants, consider team members who have different facts, opinions, and feelings. They will contribute more creative solutions to complex problems.

4. **Open-mindedness.** Participants attending the meeting will have diverse opinions. However, they need to be able to listen to one another and openly consider solutions presented by others.

Step Three: Arranging the Facility

Adequate prior planning in selecting and setting up a meeting room will contribute significantly to conducting a productive meeting. Consider the size of the room in relation to the number of participants. Will there be enough room to comfortably accommodate participants and any required furnishings and audiovisual aids?

Check to see that the heating/cooling, lighting, and ventilation are adequate for the size of your group and the activities you have planned during the meeting.

Determine seating arrangements. Generally speaking, participants attending informational meetings can be seated facing forward so that they can maintain eye contact with the group leader. They may not need tables. Participants attending decision-making meetings should be seated so that they face one another. If participants are not all familiar with one another, have name tents for team members.

The Role of the Leader

As a leader of a group, you are responsible for creating an environment in which people can and do contribute to discussions that lead to recommendations. You are in charge of creating and maintaining conditions in which people feel free to contribute, arguments are minimized, and focus remains on the objective.

Throughout the meeting, you are tasked with monitoring progress and providing the direction needed to keep participants on track. You will be continually analyzing the group's progress and refocusing the direction, if necessary, to ensure the group moves forward to meet its objective.

With practice, you can conduct a productive meeting and do it well. Consider the following tips as you mentally prepare to lead great meetings.

1. **Be prepared to lead**. Make sure that you have the agenda ready, the room arrangements made, and that you are knowledgeable about the items that will be discussed during the meeting.

2. **Believe in yourself**. Management would not have assigned you the role of group leader if they did not believe that you could handle the situation. They respect your ability.

3. **View leading as a opportunity**. View the role of group leader as an opportunity to take additional responsibility within your organization. Being a leader takes more preparation than being a participant. Welcome the required extra effort as being an opportunity to excel and do whatever it takes to prepare yourself to lead the group.

4. **Aim for excellence**. Set high standards. Expect excellent contributions from the members of your team. Lead by example. Your team members will respect you, recognize your effort, and contribute more to your meetings.

Rational Decision-Making Process

Your role as a leader of a decision-making or problem-solving meeting will require that you have an understanding of the Rational Decision-Making Process. This process provides a structured order and keeps participants' attention focused on the problem.

Step One: Analyze the Problem

First, spend time leading the group while they analyze the problem. During this time, participants will contribute their perspective about the problem or situation that has brought the group together. This is not a time for participants to suggest solutions. Ensure that all participants have the opportunity to share their views about the problem. This is important because people from different sections of the organization may view the problem from entirely different perspectives.

Step Two: Define the Problem

After all participants have had the opportunity to share their perspectives relating to the problem, define the problem. Lead the group to consensus on a clear definition of the problem. Once the problem is clearly defined, you are ready to start the process that will move the group forward to a solution or recommendation.

Step Three: State the Desired Outcome

At this point in the meeting, participants have discussed and defined the problem. It is now time to state the objective or the end result the participants want to achieve. For example, a group of supervisors may be trying to determine an equitable system for scheduling. After discussing concerns raised by employees regarding the schedule, the group determines that their objective will be to develop a schedule that gives employees an equal number of weekends and holidays off.

Step Four: Generate Alternative Solutions

There are a number of ways that alternatives can be generated. The most common is by open discussion or brainstorming. The brainstorming process is discussed below.

Step Five: Use Consensus to Reach Agreement

Although voting is appropriate for larger groups, it generally should not be used in smaller groups, particularly when participants work with one another on a day-to-day basis. Voting creates winners and losers. Although both groups will continue working together after the decision is made, the losers may have a tougher time accepting the solution reached by the group. This is understandable, because their solution wasn't the one picked. While reaching consensus is a more time-consuming process than voting, it is a process that builds group cohesiveness and commitment to reaching a workable solution.

Brainstorming Effectively

The following tips will help you use brainstorming to generate possible solutions to problems effectively.

1. **List all ideas generated by the group**. Encourage group members to contribute their ideas, even if they think that they may not be workable solutions to the problem. To ensure that everyone is heard, only one person speaks at a time.

2. **Welcome creativity**. "Off-the-wall" suggestions and comments may seem completely off target, but may provide other participants the stimulus for generating a workable solution. Off-the-wall suggestions are often the jumping off point for devising novel solutions to complex problems.

3. **Make no evaluation**. Participants must not dismiss, criticize, evaluate, or judge team members' contributions during this phase of the brainstorming process. Insist that each

167

participant listens openly to the contributions of others.

4. **Limit discussion**. The intent of the brainstorming process is to generate ideas. Do not discuss ideas at this point as it slows down and limits the brainstorming process. Discussion should only occur when another participant needs clarification on a particular idea.

5. **Encourage contributions.** The more ideas participants contribute, the more likely it is that a workable solution will be devised. Continue to list participants' ideas, even though they may be repetitious. Duplicates can be deleted later. If the group needs stimulus to continue generating ideas, think of the five W's and H—Who, What, When, Where, Why, and How.

6. **Record ideas.** Designate a recorder to write down all ideas generated, preferably on a flip chart or chalkboard so that participants can easily see all suggested solutions.

7. **Rest on decision**. Once consensus is reached and a decision made, take some time to "sleep on" the decision. What seems like a novel solution to a complex problem today may not meet the needs of all concerned tomorrow. It is best to take some time so that participants and others affected by the decision have the opportunity to think through the aspects of the proposed solution.

Ideas for Generating or Stimulating Discussion

When a group is trying to reach consensus on a solution, it is important that all the participants engage in discussion. Participants must feel comfortable and confident that their contributions will be heard. Facilitating a meeting in which participants have the confidence to contribute is challenging. Understanding the following techniques will help you lead the group in an atmosphere of free exchange and will maximize participant discussion.

1. **Ask participants what they think.** One particularly effective technique used to generate discussions is to ask members of the group to share their feelings or opinions about a particular topic. Questions such as, "What is your thinking on...?" or "What made you come to that conclusion...?" or "Would you tell me more about your thinking on...?" will all get participants involved in the discussion.

2. **Ask for more explanation.** When you don't understand a participant's contribution or you realize that members of the group aren't clear on an issue, ask for clarification. For example, "John, I'm not sure I fully understood your last comment. Could you explain it again for us?" or "Joan, this looks like it's confusing you. Would it help if Mike explained it again?"

3. **Paraphrase participants' contributions.**
   When your goal is understanding, paraphrase
   participants' responses. Questions such as, "If
   I understand it correctly, are you saying
   that...?" or "Mary, could you restate what you
   just said so that we can make sure we
   understand?" or "John is suggesting..." will all
   help the group focus on what is being said.

4. **Ask for a review of progress made.** When
   many ideas have been presented, it is a good
   idea for you to summarize the information that
   has been presented, or ask a member of the
   group to do so. For example, "We've heard a lot
   of good ideas in the past hour. Would someone
   volunteer to summarize what we have come to
   agreement on?" or "Jack, you don't seem to be
   in agreement on this point. Would you please
   summarize your major objections?"

5. **Support and encourage participants.** When
   it becomes apparent that someone is not
   contributing, you might say, "Let's give Mary a
   chance to tell us her thinking on..." or "We
   understand your suggestions, Dale. Now, let's
   ask for Tom's thoughts on..." or "Before we go
   to the next point, I'd like to get Betty's opinion
   on this."

6. **Refocus the group's attention.** Periodically,
   when the group seems to be straying off task,
   to help them refocus, ask, "Are we on the right
   track here?" or "Is this one of the goals we
   identified?" or "Are we limiting our thinking?
   Are their other ways to get this done?"

7. **Address differences of opinion.** When it becomes apparent that a group member is not in agreement, address the participant specifically. Failure to acknowledge disagreement now may cause problems in the future. "Paul, I'm sensing that you are not in agreement with this proposed solution. Could you tell us why you don't agree?" "Elaine, I think you have a differing opinion. Please tell us your thoughts on this topic."

8. **Check for group consensus.** Checking for group consensus can be done periodically throughout the meeting. This helps the group come to closure on items already discussed and focus on items still under discussion. "We've covered five items this morning. Let's check to see if we're in agreement on…" "Before we take our break, let's check to see if we agree on…" "Is this solution one that we can all accept?"

Meetings are inevitable. How you lead meetings is up to you. Following the tips provided in this chapter will help you confidently lead involving, productive meetings, meetings in which participants leave saying, "Wow! We accomplished a lot in that meeting!"

Meeting Planning Checklist

When preparing for a meeting, review the specific tasks and then check each one off as it is completed.

Specific Task	Completed
Determine whether or not a meeting needs to be held.	
Decide what type of meeting is appropriate (information/decision).	
Decide who should attend the meeting.	
Select a meeting time.	
Select a meeting place.	
Develop an agenda.	
Notify participants of the meeting.	
If participants require preparation time, send agenda beforehand.	
Arrive early to check room arrangement.	
Check to see that all A.V. equipment is operational.	
Start meeting on time.	
Review agenda with participants.	
State objective/outcome for meeting.	
Encourage participation.	
Keep group discussion focused on topic.	
Lead group to consensus.	
Summarize group progress.	
Decide what follow-up action is required.	
After meeting, write up minutes and distribute to participants.	

Tips for Success:
Meeting Facilitation

1. Before you plan to call a meeting, ask yourself this important question, "Do we need to meet, or is there a more efficient way to accomplish our goal?"

2. If a meeting is worth calling, an agenda is a must. The agenda signifies the importance of the meeting and lends structure and organization throughout the meeting.

3. Send the agenda to participants prior to the meeting, allowing them enough time to focus their thoughts and do any advance preparation prior to the meeting.

4. Arrange the facility according to the type of meeting. If discussion is required, plan to have participants face one another.

5. Begin and end meetings on time. Doing so conveys you value the participants' time and intend to use it efficiently.

6. In your opening statements, clearly state the desired outcome for the meeting.

7. Encourage participation. If you sense that there may be disagreement, even if nothing is said, have the confidence to call directly on individuals. For example, "Susan, I am feeling that you have some thoughts about this issue. Would you share them with us?"

8. Keep the discussion focused. If needed, remind participants about the goal for the meeting and redirect comments that do not relate to the current discussion.

9. Make every effort to come to agreement by consensus, not voting. Periodically check in with participants to see if they can support decisions under consideration.

10. Summarize progress and review responsibilities at the end of the meeting. Don't end until participants are sure about the next steps and their individual responsibilities.

Managing Conflict

> *"The pure and simple truth is rarely*
> *pure and never simple."*
> Oscar Wilde

As a supervisor or manager, no matter how carefully you plan, periodically you will have to deal with conflict. Wherever you have groups of people working together, you are going to experience conflict. While it is unrealistic to think that you can create a conflict-free environment, you can learn more about how to resolve issues so that conflict doesn't overwhelm you and impact your company's productivity.

The intent of this chapter is to give you the tools that you need to understand what causes conflict, how to deal with conflict, and how to keep conflict under control in your organization. With practice, you will become confident in your ability to resolve conflicts that typically arise in the day-to-day operations of an organization.

Common Misconceptions about Conflict

Many relatively successful supervisors and managers have a fear of conflict. Much of their fear stems from misconceptions about the subject of conflict. One way of diffusing that fear is to explore and shatter some misconceptions that are commonly associated with the subject of conflict. Learning more about dealing with conflict will help reduce your fear of conflict and enhance your business, family, and social contacts.

1. **If you ignore conflict, it will take care of itself.** In most cases, nothing could be further from the truth. While it may be true that in some cases you can choose to ignore conflict, recognize that this is a coping strategy, not a solution to conflict. Most often, when conflicts are ignored, things usually get worse. Generally speaking, it is best to develop a plan to deal with challenging situations and not assume that conflict will resolve itself.

2. **Conflict results from poor management.** Relationships in the workplace are diverse and subject to periods of disharmony. The effective supervisor or manager acknowledges conflict as a challenge and deals with it when it presents itself. Confident supervisors know that some tension in the workplace is normal and have a positive attitude about their ability to resolve conflict. Taking the opportunity to coach and counsel employees regarding inappropriate behavior increases your effectiveness as a manager and helps reduce potential conflict.

3. **Anger is a destructive emotion.** Anger, like other human emotions, exists and is neither positive nor negative. Anger in the workplace

176

does not have to be thought of as negative or bad. Anger only exists where there are strong emotions. If people didn't have a commitment and care about an issue, they would not exhibit anger. When anger is vented appropriately, it can help people move forward and resolve their conflict.

4. **All conflict must be resolved immediately.** In some cases, a rush towards resolution of conflict may actually limit your success. Some conflict is best managed by a series of interventions, not a quick fix.

5. **Conflict indicates low regard for the organization.** Actually, just the opposite is true. If people didn't care about their organization, they would not expend the energy. Generally, conflict occurs in areas where people have a deep concern. Conflict can help clarify emotions and serve as a tool for helping to determine an organization's core values.

Stages of Conflict

We find it helpful to view conflict in three different stages. By viewing conflict in stages, you will find it easier to determine the severity of the conflict and its impact on the organization. Once the level of conflict is determined, it becomes easier to determine a plan of action and work towards a realistic solution.

Stage One Conflict

Conflict at Stage One is real, but often not intense. Typically, people working together will have different goals, values, and unique individual needs. In Stage One conflicts, people feel discomfort and possibly annoyance, but do not get very emotional about the conflict.

In Stage One conflict, communication is typically specific and clear because the people and the problem are not intertwined. Brainstorming activities will work well at this level, because people are willing to discuss the problem specifically and leave out the personalities.

Tips to help managers and supervisors resolve Stage One conflicts include:

1. **Get employees involved to examine the conflict carefully.** Get both sides talking and ensure that they both listen to one another.

2. **Make sure that employees stick to the issues.** Don't let either party bring up emotional issues from previous conflicts. Deal only with the facts relating to this particular conflict. Ask whether their reaction is in proportion to the problem.

3. **Help employees identify points of agreement first.** Working from the points of agreement, try to identify and resolve the points of disagreement. Help employees see the big picture and get beyond their issues of conflict.

Stage Two Conflict

Conflict at the Stage Two level becomes characterized by a win/lose attitude. The wins and losses seem greater because the people involved are emotionally tied to the problem. At this level of conflict, people keep track of their verbal victories, witnesses take sides, and sides begin to keep track of their wins and losses.

Tips to help diffuse conflict at the Stage Two level include:

1. **Interview for accuracy.** Interview all parties individually so the issues are clear prior to confronting the conflict collectively. When you accurately know all the issues and perceptions, you will be in a better position to resolve or mediate the conflict.

2. **Create a neutral atmosphere.** Create a safe, neutral atmosphere in which to discuss the conflict. Seat participants in a circle, not across from one another. Seating participants close to one another, without the security of a table or desk between them, helps set the right tone for conflict resolution.

3. **Create an agenda.** Have an agenda and be responsible for keeping participants focused on its contents.

4. **Keep the group focused in the aim frame.** Groups focused in the aim frame ask two questions: "Where do want to be?" and "How do we get there?" Focusing the group on these questions will reduce finger pointing and blaming.

5. **Focus on the facts.** Take whatever time it takes to make sure that you have all the details. Make sure that you clarify any generalizations. Ask participants to clarify who *they* is and how many times *always* means.

6. **Encourage teamwork.** Each participant is equally responsible for finding an acceptable alternative to resolve the conflict.

7. **Focus on points of agreement and look for middle ground.** At this point, do not suggest compromise. Typically, people involved in Stage Two conflict are emotional. To them, a compromise may mean giving up and may feel like a loss. Keep exploring alternatives until both parties can agree on an acceptable solution.

8. **Recognize that helping people resolve conflict takes time.** Allow enough time for each party to express all their concerns regarding the conflict. Take what time is needed to find a solution to the conflict that is agreeable to all parties. Rushing or forcing a resolution may create a quick fix, but not a lasting solution to the conflict.

Stage Three Conflict

When conflict escalates to Stage Three, both being right and wanting to punish wrong become increasingly important. Sides are drawn and people rally around their cause. The conflict becomes all-consuming and parties involved make it the focus, expending a large amount of their effort and energy in their commitment to their cause.

In true Stage Three conflict, issues are intense and there is little middle ground. Sides polarize and insiders try to persuade outsiders to join their cause. Both sides enlist support by promoting their cause as being what is best for the organization. In truth, as the conflict escalates, both sides become increasingly more committed to winning and frequently lose sight of what damage their conflict is inflicting on the organization.

Tips for dealing with conflict at the Stage Three level include:

1. **Make a commitment to get all the details.**
    This will require time. It may be helpful to
    involve an objective, neutral party to do the
    investigation. Commit to interviewing as many
    people as necessary to ensure that details are
    accurate and complete. This will require sifting
    through a great deal of information clouded by
    emotion, but it is a critical step.

2. **Recognize and understand the intensity of
    individuals' commitment to their cause.**
    From an outsider's point of view, you can
    logically think through the conflict. Know that
    logic and reason will not necessarily persuade
    those personally involved in the conflict at this
    level to think differently. Concentrate on
    getting agreement on the facts and mediating a
    solution that is acceptable to both sides.

3. **Once the conflict is resolved, concentrate
    on corporate goals.** Conflict at this level is
    intense and a period of healing will be required
    after it has been resolved. Make sure that both
    sides understand the need to commit to their
    organization's goals. Redirect energies away
    from the conflict that polarized sides. Focus on
    the future and what all employees can
    contribute towards common organizational
    goals.

Conflict Stages

Stages	Characteristics of Conflict Stages
One	1. Individuals agree to meet and discuss the facts. 2. Both sides believe they can resolve the conflict. 3. Individuals can discuss the problem without involving personalities. 4. Parties involved stick to the facts and work towards a solution. 5. Individuals agree on a solution and implement it positively.
Two	1. A sense of competition exists between both sides. 2. Parties focus on "winners" and "losers." 3. The facts become obscured by personalities. 4. The language used is emotional and general. (Phrases such as "They always," "She never," and "They are such" obscure facts and intensify emotional responses to the conflict.) 5. Parties are more willing to continue the conflict for the sake of making themselves look good than they are to entertain attempts to resolve the conflict.
Three	1. Parties are obsessed with "winning." 2. Attempts are being made to "get rid" of others. 3. Sides become polarized; each side attempts to attract followers. 4. Leaders or spokespersons for each side emerge. 5. Corporate good becomes secondary to the goal of each side winning. 6. There appears to be no common ground; issues have escalated to only black and white options; solutions seem unattainable.

Handling Conflict Positively

One of the challenges of dealing with conflict is to help people maintain healthy relationships *during* and *after* periods of conflict. Simply resolving the problem is not enough. The people involved must be satisfied with the outcome and attention must be given to their emotional well-being. If these two areas are not addressed, chances are other problems will surface within time. The following tips will help you maintain healthy relationships during periods of conflict.

1. **Acknowledge conflict.** Workplace conflict happens. Effective supervisors acknowledge conflict and take steps to help employees resolve conflict.

2. **Encourage participation.** Managers and supervisors can help people overcome problems that split groups by encouraging participation. Getting involved parties to acknowledge ownership of the problem and work towards resolution helps build commitment to the good of the organization.

3. **Create a safe environment.** Creating a neutral environment in which both parties can present their facts, discuss the problem, and suggest ideas for resolving the conflict is one way to support and encourage participation leading to conflict resolution.

4. **Encourage commitment.** Reminding people that collectively "we" own the problems and collectively "we" have the power to resolve them is a good technique for encouraging commitment to ending the conflict.

5. **Question to determine the facts.** Conflict, by nature, gets emotional. Although people may not intentionally lie, their perspective colors their perception of the facts. As a leader during conflict resolution, keep listening and questioning to make sure that you have the facts straight. As people passionately present their case, this will be a challenge.

6. **Listen, listen, listen.** During periods of conflict, listening skills are critical. It costs you nothing to listen and gives you a much better perspective on the problems surrounding the conflict. As managers and supervisors, we are used to doing the talking. We feel confident when we are in charge of the conversation. As a leader dealing with conflict, however, we need to stop talking and start listening.

7. **Listen objectively.** In order to support people during conflict, don't argue with their facts. Instead, keep questioning, making sure that all parties have an opportunity to be heard before any decisions are made. Typically, when the facts are separated from the opinions, it becomes easier to think creatively and propose alternative solutions, leading to an acceptable solution to the conflict being discussed.

185

8. **Focus on the problem, not the people.** This is a challenge, because in Stages Two and Three conflict, the people and the problem are intertwined. Personalities align with one another and the details surrounding the facts or situation that originally started the conflict become obscured. As a leader, you must work hard to keep the people issues separate from the facts. Insist that parties focus on the facts. If emotions flare and parties begin attacking one another personally, steer the discussion back to the facts. Insist that parties listen to one another as they present their facts. Get agreement from both parties on the facts. Sticking to the facts plays down emotional responses and enhances the problem-solving process.

9. **Take more time to reach a decision, if necessary.** Although we are not recommending avoidance as a problem-solving technique, declaring a "timeout" at some point in the conflict resolution process may be helpful. Occasionally people become so passionate about their cause that they lose their perspective. Sometimes the facts needed to resolve a problem are not available. Leaders must communicate why they are delaying the decision so that the parties involved maintain their confidence in their leadership.

10. **Follow-up.** Initially, after conflict has been addressed and resolved, it is usual for things to appear to be going more smoothly. Don't assume this will last. Periodically check back with both parties to ask how things are going. If issues emerge, get both parties together again and address the concerns before the situation escalates.

Finally, recognize that despite all that you do to keep your leadership positive and focused on organizational goals, conflict in the workplace will be inevitable! Use what you have learned in this chapter to counsel, mediate, and lead confidently during a time of organizational conflict. Your ability to help others deal rationally with conflict will identify you as a valuable team player within your organization.

Tips for Success:
Conflict Resolution

1. If you work with people, there is potential for conflict. This is no reflection on your ability as a supervisor or manager. What will distinguish you is your ability to deal confidently with workplace conflict.

2. Don't ignore conflict. Chances are, if left alone, the conflict will escalate, not go away.

3. Before attempting to resolve issues, make sure you know the facts. The best way is to talk with employees one-on-one to learn firsthand about their perceptions regarding the conflict.

4. Remember to listen more than you speak when resolving conflict. When the conflict revolves around people and feelings, it is critical that you listen, listen, and then listen some more!

5. Make every attempt to remain objective and neutral. By staying calm, objective, and solution oriented, you are modeling positive techniques for resolving conflict.

6. To help ensure you remain objective, focus on the problem, not the people involved with the problem.

7. During periods of conflict, help employees refocus their attention on your team's goals. Emphasizing goals and outcomes demonstrates your commitment to resolving the conflict and focuses energy back on the reason your company is in business.

8. If you reach a "stalemate" when attempting to resolve conflict, declare a "time out." Giving those involved a time to "cool off" may help all parties better focus on solutions.

9. When resolving conflict, strive to achieve a solution that is mutually acceptable to all parties. The goal is to ensure that neither party in the conflict feels like the "loser."

10. Once the conflict is resolved, periodically check back with the participants to make sure that there are no further issues.

13

Creating a Motivating Environment

> *"What I do best is share my enthusiasm."*
> Bill Gates

A frequent complaint from many supervisors is that their employees lack motivation. Supervisors feel this lack of motivation is responsible for most of the problems they encounter, from tardiness to a lack of productivity. The big question is, "How do I motivate my employees?" This chapter will define motivation and explore how to use it in the workplace.

One of the first questions we need to address is, "Is it really possible to motivate anyone?" Most people will agree we can motivate ourselves, but many of us have tried a myriad of different ideas and we still have not created motivation in another person. This is because you cannot motivate anyone! What you can do is create an environment that is conducive to motivating someone. You can also create an environment that will demotivate someone.

Motivation is an internally generated phenomenon. It is a feeling that each of us develops internally

189

and it causes us to act. As supervisors, our focus should be on how we can develop an environment and a relationship with our employees that fosters the action of motivation.

What Is Motivation?

Motivation can best be described as the internal drive to fulfill a need. Each of us has specific needs. These needs translate into drives which we act upon through specific behaviors. Drives are action-oriented and provide an energizing thrust toward goal accomplishment.

As we act on the behaviors (through drives), we satisfy our needs. As our needs are satisfied, the intensity of the drive subsides. A more succinct explanation is that "people do what they think they have to do in order to get what they think they want." As supervisors, if we truly want to create motivated individuals, we have to fully understand their needs and goals. If we can understand the needs and goals of our employees, we have a good possibility of showing them the appropriate behaviors that will help them satisfy their needs. And, those appropriate behaviors will be the behaviors that satisfy our needs and goals.

There is a big difference between internally generated motivation and just getting someone to move. Technically, the term *motivation* can be traced to the Latin word *movere*, which means to move. Motivation is an *inner state* that energizes and activates—or moves—a person toward a goal.

Historically, supervisors have been quite effective in providing the external motivation to get employees to move: "If you don't work faster, you will be fired." Most likely, the employee will begin working faster because he or she does not want to lose the job. But, is the increase in productivity due to an inner push or an outside threat from the supervisor? The supervisor was able to move, not motivate, the employee. Most likely, the employee will produce just enough not to be fired, but the employee will not produce what he or she would be truly capable of if internally motivated.

Creating a Motivational Environment

The best supervisors have the most productive people who are also happy. The real challenge for supervisors is to design incentive systems that encourage high performance *and* also engender high employee morale. The following steps related to positive reinforcement will help raise levels of employee motivation.

Step One: Describe the Goal or Target Behavior

The target should always be related to performance. What specifically must the individual do to become a high performer? Answers such as work faster, be dependable, or take initiative are too general. "Answer the phone in a more professional manner" should be replaced with,

191

"When you answer the phone, say, 'This is XYZ Enterprises, Donna speaking. How may I direct your call?'" State the goal or target behavior clearly.

If the target behavior is actually a complex chain of behaviors, divide it into a chain of smaller successive behaviors. It is best to find a smaller series of steps you can reward instead of waiting to reward the individual when the entire task is completed. In other words, acknowledge small successes.

Step Two: Check the Technical Skill Level

Make sure the individual possesses the technical skill required for the job. If low performance is due to lack of natural ability or training, provide the training and information to set the employee up for success.

Step Three: Select a Meaningful Reward

Make sure that you know your employees well enough to provide an appropriate reward that will be meaningful to that person. "One size fits all" rewards are not going to motivate everyone on your team.

Step Four: Provide Positive Reinforcement

Make all positive reinforcement based on the employee moving closer to the target behavior you desire. If the employee receives the same reward at performance level two as at performance level five, the supervisor's reinforcement actually discourages improvement. This is what happens when everyone in the organization is given the same raise reward.

Step Five: Administer Immediate Rewards

Administer rewards immediately following each improvement in behavior. Most managers and supervisors give positive feedback at the worst possible time—when they want to, not when the employee would be most reinforced by it. Feedback on the negative consequences of an employee's performance is often delayed for months by the supervisor. No wonder we have problems with motivation!

Step Six: Use Intermittent Reinforcement

As the desired behavior becomes a reality, change from a continuous reward structure to an intermittent reinforcement schedule. Administering a reward every time a given behavior occurs is continuous reinforcement. Administering rewards on an intermittent basis means administering the same reward each time, but not every time it is warranted. Neither approach is clearly superior, but they both have trade-offs.

Continuous reinforcement represents the fastest way to establish new behavior. In contrast, partial reinforcement is a very slow process and it is resistant to extinction. For example, an employee

193

who is praised every time an accurate report is written will quickly learn that you value accuracy. But, what happens when you are on vacation and there is no one to offer that praise? That behavior becomes prone to extinction.

In contrast, partial reinforcement, although slow, is resistant to extinction. Gamblers in Las Vegas are excellent examples of partial reinforcement outcomes. Some people stay motivated to win long after they should have stopped an unsuccessful behavior!

Meaningful Recognition

Feeling appreciated and recognized are two of the most powerful motivators available to the supervisor. The question then becomes, "What is meaningful recognition?" Recognition is meaningful when tailored to the individual being praised. Instead of the usual "grip and grin" so many managers employ to thank someone for the job they have done, the manager should tap into the uniqueness the individual brings to the job.

One way to explain this uniqueness is to look at a painting an artist creates. This painting is a unique contribution, in many ways a gift that the artist is giving to society. If the artist is good enough, the painting might even have a commodity value.

Lewis Hyde, a poet and essayist, describes this concept when he states, "It is the cardinal difference between the gift and commodity exchange that a gift establishes a feeling-bond between two people, while the sale of a commodity leaves no connection."

If we only value and recognize the commodity side of our relationship with employees—the dollars we pay them—then we are undervaluing the uniqueness and gifted nature they bring to their jobs. Human work is not just a commodity. If we feel we are just a commodity and that anyone qualified could do our job, we begin to lose our motivation.

Our motivation intensifies when we, and others, recognize the gifted nature of our work. Try to value the uniqueness of each employee, recognizing that his or her work is a gift. Every employee has different strengths we need to recognize. We cannot forget that motivation is a feeling. Recognizing people's unique strengths helps tap into that feeling.

Recognition Suggestions

The following recognition suggestions were generated by seminar participants. It is well-documented that two of the strongest motivators available to supervisors are recognition and praise. If you are able to customize these ideas or suggestions, they will help you build a more motivated workforce and it will cost nothing more than your thoughtfulness and time.

Brainstorming Results: Ways to Recognize Employees	
Ask employees for their opinion	Bring bagels or other healthy food
Write a thank-you note to employee	Recognize or praise employee or team in a group meeting
Put a letter of recognition in employee's personnel file	Give employee a plaque or something for public display
Have your boss say thank you or send letter of appreciation to employee	Write article about accomplishments in company newsletter
Do something unexpected (buy a coffee mug, bring flowers, etc.)	Give employee time off with pay
Give a special parking place	Provide employee with business card
Award "Employee-of-the-Month"	Recognize someone via electronic mail
Award "Employee-of-the-Year"	Listen—really listen—to employee
Increase employee's responsibilities	Share a reward you receive with your employees
Recognize employee's birthday or work anniversary	Teach employee something new
Give employee a special project	Send employee to training
Take employee to lunch	Have employee train or teach others
Take employee to lunch with your boss	Have employee fill in for you during your absence
Post a memo of recognition in public area (company bulletin board)	Call to say "Job well done"
	Attach a "Post-it" that says, "Great!"

Ensuring High Motivation

There are several helpful suggestions to ensure that motivation is high in your department. You can develop an environment that makes internal motivation a reality in your employees' lives.

1. **Set high expectations with clearly-defined objectives.** When you ask people the question, "What accomplishment are you most proud of?" most will describe an accomplishment requiring significant effort to complete. Many managers think that pushing mediocre employees to higher accomplishments requires too much effort. There is no doubt, it does require tremendous effort. But, the problem with allowing mediocre or poor employees to continue at their present levels is that the cycle of low motivation also continues. There is nothing motivating about mediocre performance. It takes guts to set higher standards and then hold your employees to them. As employees rise to meet the new standards, increased feelings of motivation are fostered in the workforce.

2. **Reward people for meeting high expectations.** If you set high standards for your employees, then you need to celebrate and recognize success when achievement occurs. One of the biggest complaints from employees is that they work incredibly hard to meet deadlines, and then no one recognizes

them for their extraordinary effort. As you recognize and reward people for accomplishment, you must be sure the rewards you are bestowing are important to the recipients.

3. **Praise and recognize your employees often.** This statement sounds so easy, and yet, it is incredibly difficult to practice on a steady basis. It is easy to find things that seem more important to do, like manage the cash flow, solve a customer's problem, answer an employee's question, or complete a report. However, if time is not taken to praise and recognize your employees, motivation and morale will wane. Then, you will have a lot more things to do!

4. **Explain the "big picture."** People are motivated when they feel they are making a significant contribution to the organization. Many times, employees do not understand how significant their contribution really is. One way to demonstrate an employee's contribution is to ask the question, "What happens when the employee does not do his or her job?" Often, when the employee does not do his or her job properly, it adversely affects someone else. That someone is usually another employee, department, or customer. You need to demonstrate how each employee's contribution is connected to the overall purpose of the organization.

5. **Find out the needs and goals of your employees.** Different things motivate different people. If you are going to motivate your employees successfully, you need to find out what is motivating to each employee. Employees may be motivated by challenge, recognition, promotions, responsibility, or learning something new. Once you identify what motivates your employees, you need to merge that individual's needs and goals into your needs and goals, and then into the needs and goals of the organization.

6. **Develop your self-esteem and the esteem of others.** People with high self-esteem are more motivated and productive. We feel best about ourselves when we have been challenged and have accomplished something. This means that you constantly have to set goals for yourself. Keep your employees involved in the goal-setting process. It is important for supervisors to remember, by position alone, your behavior and actions have a tremendous impact on the way employees feel. Take the responsibility to help others feel heightened self-esteem.

7. **Get others involved in the goal-setting process.** If people are not involved in setting goals that affect their job performance, there is a strong chance that they may not be committed to the goals. Employees resent it when management sets goals that affect them without soliciting their input and then hold

them responsible for achieving those goals. The problem with a goal not being "our goal" is that we do not see the importance of achieving the goal. Therefore, it is hard to find the motivation to act on the task. We tend to spend our energies on other tasks we perceive as more important. We tend to spend our energies on our own goals.

8. **Develop a positive mental attitude.** Being around a negative person is not motivating. Negative people tend to take energy away, not instill motivation. If your attitude is negative, it is probably a reflection of your vision. If things are getting worse, what is exciting and motivating about a negative future? Be positive—people will gravitate toward you, rather than push away from you.

9. **Develop a "that's no problem" attitude.** It does not take much of a person to handle life—or a job—when everything is going right. It does take a special kind of person to handle an environment successfully when things go wrong. The most valuable employees are the ones who can look at problems and come up with solutions. They say, "We have a problem, but that's no problem." Leo Buscalia, a professor at the University of Southern California, states it best when he says, "The most successful people in life are the ones with the greatest number of viable alternatives."

200

10. **Be a positive role model.** If you want to be a motivator, you need to be motivated. You cannot demand top performance from your employees if you are unwilling to give your very best effort. When employees witness your willingness to contribute extraordinary effort, they are much more willing to go the extra mile.

Tips for Success:
Motivation

1. Remember, motivation is something internally generated. It is impossible to motivate someone else. But, you can create an environment where people find it easy to become motivated.

2. Each day, commit to looking for what is going well, and recognizing those who are responsible for that success.

3. Make the reward meaningful to the employee. People are motivated by different rewards. Tailor your praise, recognition, or other motivator to the specific recipient.

4. Link your rewards to good performance.

5. Ensure that the employee has the capabilities to do the task you are asking him or her to do.

6. Administer rewards and feedback immediately following the positive behavior you desire.

7. Choose one idea each day from "Recognition Suggestions" and pass it along to the people in your work group.

8. Maintain high expectations. Low or mediocre expectations that are accomplished are not motivating.

9. Get your employees involved in the goal-setting process. When it is also their goal, the opportunity for successful accomplishment increases.

10. Be motivated! You will never motivate anyone unless you are highly motivated yourself.

14

Setting Goals and Planning Actions

"The tragedy of life doesn't lie in not reaching your goal. The tragedy lies in having no goal to reach."
Benjamin E. Mays

In working with thousands of supervisors in diverse settings, we have noted that great leaders, among other positive characteristics, always have a set of clearly defined goals. We have also noted the reverse. Supervisors who struggle in their relationships with their employees and have difficulty getting their team motivated often have only one goal: "Just let me survive one more day!" It's a known fact that individuals and teams that set and achieve goals accomplish more, feel better about themselves, and are more confident in their abilities. Goals can be powerfully motivating.

The accomplishment of anything great begins with clear goals. There is a procedure for setting and reaching your goals. The following pages describe the goal-setting process. You will learn what it takes to be a great goal setter and goal achiever. Whether your goals are financial, business, educational, family, physical, social, spiritual, or recreational, you will be successful if you follow this process.

The Goal-Setting Process

Step One: Create a Vision

Successful leaders know the practical value of the visioning process. They also know that creating a vision is the first step in goal setting. Before you begin to set a goal, you need a clear mental *picture* of what it is you want to achieve. This picture is your vision of success. Creating a vision is the ability to see beyond *what is* to the picture of *what could be.*

To start the visioning process, you must get in touch with your true desire. What is important to you? What matters? What do you care about? What do you really want? A vision comes from the heart. It must be truly meaningful to you.
Once you are clear on what you want, begin to form the picture. Create a mental picture of what you want. Make the picture clear, specific, and detailed. See yourself in the picture. What are you doing? What are you saying? Wearing? Who else is with you? How are people treating one another? How do you feel about yourself? About the others around you?

The visioning process requires quiet reflection. Step back from your busy, fast-paced environment and relax, releasing your creativity and imagination The more relaxed you are and the farther away you are from day-to-day tensions, the easier it is to create, the easier it is to visualize. The ability to see yourself successfully achieving your goal is a critical first step in the goal-setting process.

Step Two: Decide on Actions

Now that your vision is clear, you can begin to determine the actions that must be taken to achieve the vision. These actions become the specific goals that are to be accomplished. A goal is a target, an end, or an objective. It is the accomplishment of these targets—or goals—that brings you closer to your vision.

For example, if your vision is to achieve a more prominent position in your organization or to move higher on your career path, you would first go through the visioning process and become crystal clear on what it is you actually want. You would know exactly what it would look like and how it would feel. Then ask yourself, "What do I need to accomplish to get to my vision?" One action may be to go back to school and complete a degree program. If you need the degree to achieve the vision, it becomes one of your key goals.

Step Three: Identify Roadblocks

Now that you know what it will take to achieve your vision by outlining key actions or goals, you can begin to identify the barriers or roadblocks that may get in your way. It may sound negative to spend your time and energy thinking about barriers or problems, but there are two good reasons for this:

First, if you are able to think about what problems could stop you, you can also begin to generate

205

plans to get around the problems if they should arise. And second, when they do come up, they do not paralyze you. Many people have had their goals undermined when problems surfaced. Sometimes people will even tell you they thought the problems would arise.

Back to our example of going back to school to get your degree...Some of the roadblocks you could anticipate in this goal might include (1) not enough time, (2) fear of going back to being a student, and/or (3) financial constraints. For each of the roadblocks you identify, develop some strategies to get around the problem. They may include (1) changing your own thinking, (2) getting help from others, and (3) committing to specific time blocks to do what you need to do. Keep the vision in mind and then overcoming the roadblocks will not be so tough.

Step Four: List the Benefits

If you spend time listing the problems or roadblocks you could encounter, you will find it much easier to generate a list of benefits you would receive when you achieve the goal. The question that then needs to be answered is, "Do the benefits make the goal worth achieving?" If the answer is *yes*, you know that it is worth tackling the problems to achieve the benefits of goal attainment.

Continuing with our example, some of the benefits of going back to school and obtaining a degree might be (1) improved chances for promotion, (2) increased salary, (3) enhanced self-esteem, and (4) the feeling of accomplishing something you have wanted for many years.

As you list the benefits, you will want to make sure the benefits outweigh the problems you will encounter. If the benefits do not outweigh the problems, the problems will stop you. Focus on the benefits. They will help you get through the tough times!

Step Five: Write the Goal

The research on high achievers shows that successful goal setters write out their goals. There is something almost magical about writing down goals. Without writing down the goal, it is merely an idea or a wish. Writing it down helps to bring it to life.

Here is a simple, yet effective guideline for writing good goals. It is called the **S-M-A-R-T** model. Each letter of the **S-M-A-R-T** model refers to a characteristic of effective goals:

Specific. Good goals are specific. They detail exactly what is to be accomplished. Don't be vague or general. Write out specifically what is to be accomplished.

Measurable. You must be able to measure the success of your goal. In other words, how will you know when you are successful? Whether the goal is broken down into number of units produced, salary earned, days worked, pounds lost, chapters completed, or number of classes attended, you need a way to quantify your results. Measuring your results helps to keep you moving toward your goal. Yes, it is a great motivator!

Attainable. Research shows us that high achievers set goals that challenge their abilities, but that are not unrealistically out of reach. When you set challenging, but attainable goals, you will experience success and increase your self-esteem. Be realistic about your goals. It is not unrealistic to go back to school for a degree. It is unrealistic to expect to get a doctorate in only one year. Make your goals a stretch, but make them a more guaranteed stretch!

Relevant. Do not forget that your vision is the driver for your goals. Make sure that your goals are relevant to the vision. The accomplishment of each goal should move you closer to realizing your vision. Keep your goals moving on the track to your desired future.

Time bound. Good goals have a time frame. When you set a specific time frame to get something done, it will always take you that amount of time or even less time to complete the task than if you had no time frame at all. For example, when you prepare go on vacation, you have all sorts of tasks that need to be accomplished before you leave. You may be rushed, but you will always get the tasks done. You have to because you are leaving. If you were not leaving, those same tasks might take you two or three times as long to accomplish. Life is short! Set a time frame because you will always accomplish more.

Step Six: Design an Action Plan

Now that you have your goals and they are **S-M-A-R-T** goals, you know exactly what you want to achieve and by when. The last step in the goal-setting process is to design a specific action plan to achieve the goals. This is a step-by-step breakdown of the small actions you will take to achieve each goal and when you will take them.

Back to the degree example. Let's say your goal is stated like this:

> *I will complete my M.S. degree by December 2001.*

Your specific action plan might look like the one on the next page.

Each time you complete an action, check it off or scratch it out and then celebrate. You are on your way to achieving your ultimate goal!

Goal: To complete my M.S. degree by December 2001		
Specific Actions	**By What Deadline**	**Completed**
1. Call the university and get an application	May, this year	
2. Call my former college so transcripts can be sent	June, this year	
3. Complete application and send it in	July 15, this year	
4. Set up meeting with university counselor	August 1, this year	
5. Register for classes	August 22, this year	

Remember, the secret to achieving goals is your willingness to do whatever it takes to get there. It means that you are willing to sacrifice to accomplish your goal. It means that you are willing to confront problems and roadblocks and work around them. It means that you will write out your goals and ensure that they are **S-M-A-R-T**. It takes work. And, it also means that you will reap the benefits—that you will bring your vision to life!

A sample format for setting detailed and specific goals is provided on the next few pages.

Goal Setting Action Plan

1. **Is my vision crystallized? ____Yes ____No
    (Can I clearly see myself achieving this goal?)**

2. **Describe the goal:** _____

    _____

    _____

3. **What problems could stop me from
    achieving this goal?**

    _____

    _____

    _____

4. **What are the benefits of achieving this
    goal?** _____

    _____

    _____

    _____

    _____

    _____

5. **What is my plan to overcome the problems I listed in question #3?**

    _____

    _____

    _____

    _____

    _____

    _____

    _____

6. **When will I complete this goal (specify date)?** _____

7. **What are the milestone markers? (What will be evidence that I am getting closer to completing my goal?)**

    WHAT   **BY WHEN**

    _____   _____

    _____   _____

    _____   _____

    _____   _____

8. How will I measure this goal? _____

_____

_____

9. Is the goal realistic and attainable?
   ____Yes   ____No

10. If others are responsible for accomplishing
    this goal, have I involved them in setting
    the goal? ____Yes   ____No

11. What can I do to help others feel ownership
    of this goal? _____

_____

_____

12. What is my action plan to achieve this
    goal?

    WHAT   **BY WHEN**

    _____   _____

    _____   _____

    _____   _____

    _____   _____

    _____   _____

Setting Goals with Employees

If you are setting goals that involve your employees, here are some suggestions that will help you create successful goals that employees will feel motivated to achieve.

1. **Involve employees in the goal-setting process.** One of the classic pitfalls supervisors stumble into is setting goals *for* their employees versus *with* their employees. People want to contribute to the goals for which they will be held accountable. Dumping your goals on employees without their input is a de-motivator. Have your employees create their goals with you. You will be surprised at the level of commitment and personal ownership you will see.

2. **Ask how the employee can accomplish the goal before you tell how.** Ask your employees for their ideas on how to accomplish the goal before you give your input. If you get their input on how the goal can be accomplished, you may get some new, creative, and better approaches. The key here, as with all good communication, is to listen.

3. **Ensure the goal's feasibility.** If you set a goal with your employees to have the departmental budget completed by the end of the month, you must make sure the employees have access to the tools and information they need to complete the task. Set your employees

up for success by ensuring they have what they require to do the job. This goes back to making sure that the goal is realistic and attainable.

4. **Make the goal challenging.** Tasks that are not challenging are not motivating. One of the most fundamental motivations for any employee, especially one who is basically competent at his or her work, is challenge. Challenge creates motivation to achieve goals. If you allow mediocrity to continue in your department, you are undermining your own success.

5. **Ensure that the goal is relevant.** Most people do not want to accomplish a goal just for the sake of accomplishing a goal. They want to understand the purpose or why they are doing a particular task. Employees need to understand how the tasks they are doing are connected to the larger purpose of the organization. People will extend themselves for work they see as important. Make sure you take the time to explain the importance or relevance of the goal. Remember, good goals are relevant.

6. **Recognize success.** Make sure to recognize your employee's success. We all want to know that our work is acknowledged and recognized. This does not take much time but will buy you a great deal. Employees want to please supervisors. Take the time to acknowledge

them with a written note, a pat on the back, or a simple "good job," and you will have a cadre of loyal, hard-working employees.

In conclusion, setting and achieving goals can be incredibly motivating, both personally for you and for your team. Goals give you a well-defined purpose, a sense of accomplishment, and a feeling of mastery over your environment. Without goals, you are like a ship without sails and a rudder, at the mercy of the wind. You will drift, but not drive. Set goals, commit to the hard work it takes to achieve your goals, and chart your own course!

Tips for Success:
Goals and Actions

1. Set goals. Most people do not set goals. Those that do are far more likely to accomplish what they want in life.

2. Adopt a positive attitude. People who achieve significant results and a sense of fulfillment in their lives view the glass as half full instead of half empty.

3. Do it now. Successful goal setters take action *now*. Remember, the most important step in overcoming procrastination is the first step, no matter how small.

4. Clarify your vision. What do you truly want? Create a clear and specific mental picture. Use this vision to guide you in the goal-setting process.

5. Write S-M-A-R-T goals (Specific, Measurable, Attainable, Relevant, and Time-bound).

6. Design a specific action plan with target dates for completion.

7. Get your employees involved in the goal-setting process. Their involvement will foster significant personal motivation.

8. Be sure the goal is possible. Does the person have the tools and information necessary for successful completion of the goal?

9. Discuss the significance of the goal. Believe it is a goal that should be accomplished.

10. Recognize success. Any achievement deserves recognition. Whether it is a personal, team, or employee accomplishment, take time to acknowledge and recognize success.

Earning Followers in Your Leadership Role

"Management techniques are obviously essential, but what matters is leadership. Leading the whole organization needs wisdom and flair and vision and they are another matter; they cannot be reduced to a system and incorporated into a training manual."
Anthony Jay

The title makes an interesting point. It is difficult to be considered a leader if you have no followers. What makes this point so significant is that you *can be* a supervisor or manager and have no followers—all you need is employees. To take this point one step further, you can still be considered a supervisor, even if you are ineffective in your ability to direct the actions of your employees. But, this is simply not the case for a leader. A leader must have followers.

Leader or Supervisor?

Over the last 20 years, there have been countless attempts to define and differentiate leadership and management. Some have made statements such as "managers manage things, whereas leaders lead people" or "management is about efficiency, but leadership is about effectiveness." Other differentiations have stated that leaders possess "charismatic" or "heroic" qualities that allow them to influence people to positive change. In contrast, managers maintain the status quo.

A typical list of the differences between a leader and a manager/supervisor was generated by a group of participants at several of our seminars. The compiled information is outlined below.

Differences between Leader and Manager/Supervisor

Leader	Manager or Supervisor
Builds Trust	Manages Things
Motivates	Controls
Empowers People	Maintains Power
Develops Vision	Assigns Goals
Has Integrity	Plans
Develops Commitment	Demands Compliance
Coaches and Counsels	Disciplines
Asks	Tells

When people look at this list, there is no question in their minds which role they would like to play in the organization. They want to be the leader! But, in reality good managers and good leaders will probably rely on both sets of skills or behaviors at different times.

220

There is, however, one significant difference between a leader and a manager that needs to be addressed, and that deals with where their power source is based.

Leadership, unlike management, is not a formal position. It is a relationship. Managers receive their power and authority from the organization. This is what we call legitimate or position power. Leaders may hold no position power. Their power base comes voluntarily from the followers.

Ideally, we would like both of these power bases to be harvested by one person. That is, the manager is also the leader. The goal for all of us would be to perfect the skills and traits of both the leader and the manager. When we have power sourced from both directions, we have the ultimate opportunity to create positive change for our organizations.

The bottom line is that leadership and management are two distinctive and complementary systems of action. Both are necessary for success in our increasingly complex business environment. To understand more about these power bases, read below about the different types of power.

Types of Power

There are four distinctly different types of power a leader or manager may possess. Each type of power has different qualities and carries different weights in our efforts to lead people.

Type One: Power of Position

This is formal authority which gives you the sacred right to tell someone else to do something. There are times when we do not agree with our boss and we may even state our disagreement to him or her. But, then we go ahead and bow to our boss's demands. We may have responded to the power of the position. Most people respond to this power base because they practice a simple management concept called, "I want to keep my job!"

Type Two: Power of Competence

To be successful as a leader or manager, you need the competence to do the job. Competencies are gained through industry and organizational knowledge, relationships in the firm and industry, reputation and track record, and even formal schooling. The more competent others perceive us, the more likely they will be to follow us.

Type Three: Power of Personality

If you have ever worked with someone who has rubbed you the wrong way, then you know the power of a personality. Personality defines the specific skills and behaviors you utilize to help build relationships. The easier it is for others to talk to you, listen to you, and work with you, the easier it will be for them to respond to your wishes.

Type Four: Power of Character

This component is your "credit rating." Do the people you interact with perceive you as trustworthy, credible, and honest? Do they perceive you as having high personal morals, being sincere, and possessing strong ethics? You acquire this power from the trail of promises you have kept and the expectations you have fulfilled or exceeded. To put this another way, you have done what you said you were going to do and therefore people trust you.

As we look at these four bases of power, one is clearly managerial—the power of position. The other three fit under the realm of leadership. But, these three components also need to be developed simultaneously by managers and supervisors. Of the four components, the power of character is the most powerful of all. If people do not trust you or do not perceive you as credible, it will affect every other aspect of your relationship.

We have looked at the value of the four types of power and we have also discussed the importance of both managing and leading. Now, let's take a look at what we consider to be more "managerial-oriented" activities as well as activities considered to be more "leadership-oriented."

Managerial-Oriented Activities

Management, by definition, is getting things done through others. The science of management developed during the 20th century because organizations grew incredibly large. Without order and consistency, outputs such as quality, productivity, and profitability are adversely affected. To control these outputs, "managerial" functions such as planning, budgeting, organizing, staffing, controlling, and problem solving are critical. As much has been written about the technical aspects of managerial activities, we will move on to discuss leadership-oriented activities.

Leadership-Oriented Activities

While management focuses on coping with complexity, leadership is about creating positive change. Part of the reason leadership has become such a needed quality in the last 20 years is because of the rapid changes and innovation we discussed in the first chapter. The net result of these changes is that doing what was done yesterday—or even doing it 15% better—is no longer a prescription for success. Major changes are necessary to survive and compete effectively in today's environment.

To help you focus on ways to ensure you have followers to lead, we have summarized aspects critical to your leadership development.

Developing a Vision

Leading an organization, whether it is a company or a small work unit, to positive change begins with developing a vision. A vision is a clear mental picture of a desired future outcome. If you have ever put together a large 1,000-piece jigsaw puzzle, the chances are you used the picture on the top of the puzzle box to guide the placement of the pieces. That picture on the top of the box is the end result or the vision of what you are trying to turn into a reality. It is much more difficult—if not impossible—to put the jigsaw puzzle together without ever looking at the picture. An organization without a vision is like a person trying to put together a jigsaw puzzle without ever seeing the picture on the box.

Effective leaders will create and articulate a clear vision for their organization or unit. A good vision is clear and compelling. It works like a magnet, pulling people toward it.

There are at least four benefits of a clear vision.

1. **It ensures that all employees are moving in the same direction.** This means that all employees are working towards the same end result.

2. **It helps to overcome adversity.** Employees are more willing to tackle problems that get in the way of achieving the vision.

3. **It helps to create motivation.** If the leader is committed to and excited about his or her vision, the excitement is contagious. Employees will be more motivated to work

225

toward the vision and will tend to focus on the positive rather than dwell on the negative.

4. **It provides a guide for decision making.** A clear vision will help employees determine the right path when it comes to problem solving and decision making.

Aligning People

In management, we staff the organization to fulfill certain functions. Leadership involves connecting and aligning people to the true purpose of the organization. This means communicating the vision and helping the employees see how they fit into the vision. The employee is a piece of the puzzle and he or she helps to create the overall picture. He or she needs to know how critical each piece is to the overall success of the organization.

Motivating People

Good leaders create a motivating environment. They articulate the vision and help align employees to the role they play in fulfilling the vision. They also give employees the power to be involved and make decisions that affect their work. Leaders solicit and value the feedback of their employees. And, leaders help employees realize the vision by providing coaching, feedback, and role modeling. These activities help employees grow professionally and personally, which enhances their confidence and self-esteem.

Empowering People

By definition, empowerment means to give another person the authority and power to act. This means that the employees who work for you actually have the ability to get things done themselves. The opposite of empowerment is "micro-management." When we "micro-manage," we oversee every action and decision our employee makes.

To empower your staff, you must understand that power is not "zero-sum" based. Zero sum means that there is only a certain amount of power to go around, and if I give up power, I lose, and someone else gains. Thus, if I gain power, then you lose power.

The problem with seeing power as a finite source is that you spend your time and energy protecting what power you do have. This is time that could be more productively spent turning your vision into a reality or motivating your staff.

The goal is to gain the confidence and understanding that when you empower others, you are taking a risk, developing trust, and creating an enlarged power base. In a sense, you are giving away power to gain power.

The opposite is also true. If you do not trust your employees, if you do not give them the capacity to act, then they will most likely not invest their power in you or your vision. By not giving away power to your employees, you lose your own power.

Clarifying Values

The values that you carry with you are the basis for governing your decisions and behaviors. Values influence the relationships you enter into, the careers you develop, the family you raise, and millions of other decisions you are faced with each day. In many ways, values are like a moral compass that guides you through life. As a leader, it is important to clarify what values your organization or department is going to represent. What will you be known and remembered for?

When espoused values (words) and values in use (actions) meet and are consistent, you demonstrate integrity. If espoused values and actions do not meet or are in conflict, you demonstrate hypocrisy.

Building Trust

It sounds so simple: all you have to do is build trust with your employees. But, we know that this is no easy task. The following five points are some suggestions on how you can develop trust.

1. **Do what you say you are going to do.** When you tell people you are going to do something and then do not do it, or do something different, people begin to doubt your word. Do what you say you will do and you will gain credibility and trust.

2. **Provide just a little more than expected.** Whether it is additional support and

228

counseling for an employee, going the extra mile for a customer, or going a little out of your way to help a co-worker or fellow supervisor, exceeding others' expectations builds trust and loyalty.

3. **Be consistent.** If you are consistent, people can predict what actions you will take. When people are unsure of how you will act or react, they tend to proceed cautiously, or not at all.

4. **Increase responsibility.** One of the fastest ways to build trust with people is to increase their responsibility. By increasing someone's responsibility, you are taking a risk. When you take a risk and people fulfill or exceed your expectations, you develop trust in them. Your trust in them fosters their trust in you. It is a reciprocal relationship, and it is critical for good business and personal relationships.

5. **Accept honest mistakes.** Supervisors and managers tend to forget that their value lies in their experience. Their experience comes from making mistakes and learning how to proceed so the same mistakes do not happen again. If we do not have the capacity to accept mistakes, then people in our area of influence will refuse to make decisions or take risks.

Mentoring

Mentoring is just a fancy word for a coach. The power of mentoring is two-fold. It not only builds

229

up the esteem of the person being mentored, it also builds the esteem of the mentor. The reason this concept works so well is that most of us have a deep-seated need to help someone else. By helping someone else grow, we feel good in the process. And, to share something we know costs us very little except our time.

Willingness to Learn

If leadership is about creating positive change in the organization, then being a leader is about continuous learning. As fast as things are changing, it is almost impossible to maintain any type of expertise. As long as we have a willingness and desire to learn, we have the ability to adapt to new environments.

Becoming a Better Leader

There are many practical reasons for becoming a better leader. After reading the following paragraphs, you will be able to cite additional ideas that are even more relevant to your work structure.

1. **Recognize the world is rapidly changing.** Global competition, increased customer demands, and the rapid increase of information and technologies, mandate constant change. Many managers in large organizations are finding change is the one thing they can count on. Your ability to adapt to change will significantly impact your organizational success.

230

2. **Develop a positive mental attitude.** No one wants to follow someone with a rotten attitude. Enough said!

3. **Focus on what you can change...**not on what you cannot change. Where are you going to spend your energy? Complaining about things you cannot change or creating the things you can? If you feel your destiny is in someone else's hands, you do not have to take responsibility for your actions. Focus on what you can do and take responsibility. There is power in responsibility.

4. **Lead with your heart and head.** We recently heard a manager say that he did not care about people's emotions. He went on to say, "We have a job to get done!" Unfortunately, people are the ones who are going to get that job done. And, people have feelings. In fact, everything about motivation and the desire to do good work is based on a feeling. If we do not consider people's feelings, it is impossible to be an effective leader.

5. **Reach out to people who have different perspectives.** It is easy to communicate with people who think just like you. It is difficult to effectively communicate with someone who has a differing viewpoint. But, if we only have the ability to communicate with people who think like us, we are limiting ourselves from learning new and valuable information.

231

6. **Become comfortable with the unknown.**
   One of the necessities to becoming empowered
   is to feel comfortable with the unknown. This
   is called having the ability to deal with
   ambiguity. As fast as our environment is
   changing, it is impossible to know all the facts
   or have all the answers all the time. If you
   think you know everything, you are obsolete.

7. **Develop a leadership "tool kit."** No one can
   have all the answers. What you can develop is
   a "tool kit" of resources that can help to solve
   problems. If you only have a hammer, you
   tend to see every problem as a nail. Collect
   information, and then learn and practice
   leadership and management techniques.
   Remember, good leaders never stop learning.

8. **Look for multiple right answers.** With
   information and the environment changing as
   rapidly as it is, we can no longer afford to look
   unilaterally for one right answer. Become
   multilateral in your thinking. Search for
   possibilities—not just one solution.

9. **Substitute effectiveness for perfectionism.**
   If you wait until all the available information is
   in to make your decisions, the chances are you
   have waited too long. In today's environment,
   we no longer can afford the luxury of waiting
   until something is absolutely perfect. We need
   to ask the question, "What's the goal or
   purpose?" If we can satisfy the goal, then we
   are effective.

10. **Develop the flexibility of a sapling.** In San Diego, we have huge, beautiful eucalyptus trees. Unfortunately, it seems like every time there is a rain or windstorm, some of the biggest trees blow over. Fortunately, eucalyptus trees are great at dropping seeds that start new saplings. What is amazing is that the wind and the rain do not bother the saplings. They are pliable and just blow with the wind. The large trees are not so adaptable. They snap because they are not able to sway with the changing wind. In today's environment, supervisors need to be like saplings.

In closing, true leaders understand that success does not depend on their titles, but on the values they uphold and the choices they make on a daily basis. True leaders know that leadership is not achieved through technical expertise, but rather is based on an emotional connection or relationship with followers. It is our hope that the insights we presented in the previous chapters will help you with both the technical expertise and "people smarts" you need to be not only a great supervisor, but an outstanding leader!

Tips for Success:
Leadership

1. Recognize that leadership is not a formal position, it is a relationship. If you want to be a leader, you need to earn followers.

2. To be effective, you need to have strong skills in both areas—leadership *and* management.

3. As a leader, your greatest source of power comes from your character. The more others trust you, the more power you will have.

4. Create a compelling, positive vision for yourself as a leader and for your work group. A vague vision is not motivating to you or to your people.

5. Help your employees see how they contribute to bring the vision to reality.

6. Empower your employees. Give them the freedom to act and make decisions as necessary to get the job done.

7. Clarify the values you will use to guide you and your work group. Values are the basis for governing your decisions and behaviors.

8. Increase responsibilities for your employees. If you are doing your job, your employees should be growing by taking on added responsibilities.

9. Develop a willingness to learn. With the economy and environment rapidly changing, you need to be continuously learning and relearning.

10. Reach out to people who have different perspectives. If you surround yourself with people who think just like you do, eventually your work group's strengths will become their own weakness.

Bibliography

Bennis, Dr. Warren. *On Becoming a Leader.* Reading, MA: Addison-Wesley Publishing Co., 1989.

Bennis, Dr. Warren, and Nanus, Burt. *Leaders, The Strategies for Taking Charge.* New York: Harper & Row, Publishers, Inc., 1985.

Block, Peter. *The Empowered Manager: Positive Political Skills at Work.* San Francisco, CA: Jossey-Bass, 1987.

Branden, Nathaniel. *How to Raise Your Self-Esteem.* New York: Bantam Books, 1988.

California Department of Fair Employment and Housing, *DFEH-161*, State of California, 5/97.

Raines, Claire, *Beyond Generation X.* Landam, MD: Crisp Publications, 1997.

Sheehy, Gail. *Pathfinders.* New York: Bantam Books, 1982.

U.S. Bureau of the Census. *Current Population Reports, series P-25, No. 990 in the Statistical Abstract of the United States,* 1987.

U.S. Bureau of Labor Statistics. *Handbook of Labor Statistics,* June 1985.

Index

About the Authors

Peter Barron Stark specializes in leadership and management training (PBS & Associates, Inc.). For ten years, he owned his own commercial printing company and was able to use these supervisory skills with his employees. Today, he is principal of his own management consulting firm, doing business with organizations throughout the United States and abroad, presenting over 250 seminars, speeches, and workshops annually. As an instructor at San Diego State University, he also shares these principles with students.

Peter has authored two other books: *Goal Setting: Creating Your Life's Dream and Turning It into a Reality* and *It's Negotiable: The How-to Handbook of Win/Win Tactics*. He has been published in *CPA Today* and *Vital Speeches of the Day*, and he writes his own quarterly newsletter, *The Manager's Advisor*.

Jane Flaherty is a Senior Consultant with PBS & Associates. She has over 25 years' experience designing and implementing organizational interventions for the public and private sector. Prior to joining PBS & Associates in 1994, she held positions with the Department of Defense Dependents Schools, ranging from classroom teacher, to school improvement coordinator, to school principal. In addition to organization development activities, she conducts hundreds of workshops and seminars annually.

Jane serves on the faculty at San Diego State University. Her work with a diverse client base includes major and small to mid-size corporations, manufacturing firms, service organizations, government, and educational institutions.